The Dreams and Visions of
Aelius Aristides

Perspectives on Philosophy and Religious Thought

10

Perspectives on Philosophy and Religious Thought (formerly Gorgias Studies in Philosophy and Theology) provides a forum for original scholarship on theological and philosophical issues, promoting dialogue between the wide-ranging fields of religious and logical thought. This series includes studies on both the interaction between different theistic or philosophical traditions and their development in historical perspective.

The Dreams and Visions of Aelius Aristides

A Case-Study in the History of Religions

John Stephens

gorgias press
2013

Gorgias Press LLC, 954 River Road, Piscataway, NJ, 08854, USA

www.gorgiaspress.com

Copyright © 2013 by Gorgias Press LLC

All rights reserved under International and Pan-American Copyright Conventions. No part of this publication may be reproduced, stored in a retrieval system or transmitted in any form or by any means, electronic, mechanical, photocopying, recording, scanning or otherwise without the prior written permission of Gorgias Press LLC.

2013

ISBN 978-1-4632-0232-3

ISSN 1940-0020

```
Library of Congress Cataloging-in-Publication
Data

Stephens, John, 1951-
  The dreams and visions of Aelius Aristides :
a case-study in the history of religions / by
John Stephens.
       pages cm. -- (Perspectives on
philosophy and religious thought, ISSN
1940-0020)
  Includes bibliographical references and
index.
  ISBN 978-1-4632-0232-3
 1.  Aristides, Aelius--Criticism and
interpretation. 2.  Asklepios (Greek
deity)--Cult. 3.  Religion--History.  I. Title.
  PA3874.A7Z5 2013
  292.4'2092--dc23
2013029026
```

Printed in the United States of America

TABLE OF CONTENTS

Table of Contents v
Acknowledgments vii
Part One: Religio-Historical Considerations 1
Chapter One: Aristides and his Book of Dreams 3
    Introduction 3
    The Nature of Religious Experience 6
    Reasons for the study of individual religious experience 7
    Aristides' Dream-Diary: The Sacred Tales 9
    Aristides' Ancient Biographers 12
    Aristides' Modern Biographers 14
    Methodological Questions 24
Chapter Two: The Literary Dimension of the Text 27
    Aristides: An Example of Homo Religiosus 27
    The Sacred Tales and Ancient Autobiography 29
    Ancient Visionary Literature 35
Chapter Three: The Problem of Individuality in the Sacred Tales: Comparing the Sacred Tales with Other Selected Ancient Christian and Pagan Autobiographical Documents . 41
    Aristides, the Healthy-minded Versus St. Augustine, the Sick Soul 41
    Pagan and Christian Sick Souls: Marcus Aurelius and St. Paul 49
    The Sacred Tales In Comparison To the Metamorphoses 53
Chapter Four: Dreams and Miracles in the Sacred Tales 61
    The Sacred Tales and Religious Aretalogy 61
    The Sacred Tales and Early Christian Miracle Stories 71
Chapter Five: Aristides and the Religious Climate of Late Antiquity 81
    True Believers in the Greco-Roman World 81
    Skeptics and Doubters in Ancient Times 85

Systems of Dream Interpretation in the Sacred Tales and Elsewhere 87
Part Two: Psychological Considerations 93
Chapter Six: Analysis of the Manifest Contents of Aristides' Dreams 95
    The Manifest Contents of Aristides' Dreams 95
    Anthropological Approaches to the Dream 96
    Applying a Quantitative Approach to the Dreams of Aristides 98
    Frequency of Dream Images in the Sacred Tales 102
    Ancient Greek Dream Literature and the Sacred Tales 104
Chapter Seven: A Functional Analysis of the Personal Religion of Aelius Aristides 109
    A Psycho-social Perspective 109
    The Psychological Value of Aristides' Adhesion to the Cult of Asclepius 117
    The Paradoxical Divine Prescriptions 119
    Reductionist Studies of the Past 120
    Taking the Relativist Approach 123
Chapter Eight: An Analysis of the Latent Contents of Aristides' Dreams 129
    The Cross-cultural Application of Psychoanalysis 129
    The Psychoanalytic Interpretation of Aristides' Religiosity and Dreams 132
Chapter Nine: Concluding Remarks 147
Bibliography 151
Index 153
    Ancient Sources 153
    Biblical References 156
    General Index 156

ACKNOWLEDGMENTS

I would like to thank Prof. Birger Pearson, Department of Religious Studies, UC Santa Barbara for his advice and support in completing the research for this book. I am also grateful to the staff of Gorgias Press, especially Melonie Schmierer-Lee and Hoda Mitwally, for their assistance in preparing this book for publication. I would also like to express my thanks to Denise Bryan for her encouragement and all of the helpful suggestions. This book is dedicated to my three children; Danica, Elizabeth and Christopher.

PART ONE: RELIGIO-HISTORICAL CONSIDERATIONS

CHAPTER ONE: ARISTIDES AND HIS BOOK OF DREAMS

INTRODUCTION

In recent times, Aelius Aristides and his religious diary, the *Sacred Tales* have drawn a great deal of interest from a host of biblical scholars and classical historians. Aristides' religiosity offers students of early Christianity insight into the pagan religious environment at the time Christianity was spreading into the Roman world. This book conducts a thorough examination of the religious experience of Aristides, looking at both the positive and negative scholarly criticism regarding this second century CE pagan sophist and his piety. Rather than taking a negative approach (as some scholars have in the past), we will suggest a more positive approach for viewing his religious diary as well as the religious experiences described therein. In general, Aristides' pagan religiosity has been frequently misunderstood because of a certain Judeo-Christian scholarly bias against this type of pagan religious experience. Rather than seeing Aristides as an "anxious pagan" or a "sick soul," his religiosity should be judged on its own terms. Aristides represents a type of religiosity characterized by an optimistic spiritual outlook. Aristides is the "Not-So-Anxious Pagan."

Chapter One presents a definition of religious experience as well as reasons for studying individual religious experience, offering an introductory description of the contents of the *Sacred Tales* and the cult of Asclepius, and relevant information concerning Aristides' ancient and modern biographers. We will consider the various positive and negative scholarly opinions regarding Aristides' piety and conclude the discussion by assessing the "rhetorical" interpretation of the *Sacred Tales*.

Chapter Two examines the literary dimension of the text. In this context, we will argue that Aristides an example of *homo religiosus* and that his religious experience is authentic. Similar examples of ancient visionary writings are discussed and comparisons are made between the *Sacred Tales* and the writings of Thessalos of Tralles, Perpetua of Carthage, the Shepherd of Hermas and Zosimus of Panapolis.

In Chapter Three, certain types of religious experiences described in the *Sacred Tales* are compared to the religiosity articulated in the *Confessions* of St. Augustine, the *Meditations* of Marcus Aurelius, the writings of St. Paul and Book XI of the *Metamorphoses*. Using concepts derived from William James' typology of religious experience, Aristides is presented as an example of the healthy-minded religious individual whereas Augustine will be shown to be an example of the sick soul. References are also made to other pagan and Christian sick souls and healthy-minded individuals besides Aristides and some of these references include Marcus Aurelius, St. Paul and Lucius.

In Chapter Four, the miracles recorded in the *Sacred Tales* are discussed. For a variety of reasons, the *Sacred Tales* can be interpreted as an instance of the ancient literary category known as *religious aretalogy*. Although Aristides is not an example of a *theos aner*, he uses many of the same terms found in ancient miracle literature. Likewise, mystery-religion terminology is also found in the *Sacred Tales*. In this context, parallels between the NT miracle stories and the *Sacred Tales* are examined, including the NT miracle story of the woman with a hemorrhage (Mark 5:25–34), and parallels are identified between it and motifs in the *Sacred Tales*. Other typical features of the miracle story are also discussed, including the motif of the failure of the human doctors, the "paradoxical" nature of miraculous cures, and the suddenness of the miraculous cure, all of which are present in the *Sacred Tales*.

Chapter Five examines the general religious climate of the Greco-Roman world, situating the piety of Aristides against the background of the general religious environment in the Hellenistic world, especially during the Roman period. One issue considered regards the typicality of Aristides' religiosity. In this context, Alexander of Abonoteichus is presented as an example of a *theos aner*. Various systems of dream interpretation—including those developed by Artemidorus—are also surveyed. Skeptical views regarding divination are highlighted through the opinions of Cicero. Against this background of faith and doubt in antiquity, Aristides appears as one of the more extreme and intense cases of religious faith in the Greco-Roman world.

Part Two of this book discusses psychological factors involved in Aristides' piety. Chapter Six employs principles from modern anthropological studies of dreams to analyze the contents of Aristides' dreams, applying a cross-cultural quantitative method which seeks to identify patterns and re-occurring themes in the manifest content of Aristides' dreams.

This discussion is followed in Chapter Seven with a functional analysis of the personal religion of Aristides, understanding Aristides' conversion to Asclepius from a modern psychological perspective. Erikson's psycho-social model of the mind is applied to Aristides. Aristides' pagan conversion is compared to Augustine's Christian conversion and other examples of pagan quasi-conversion are discussed including that described by Dio of Prusa. The psychological function of Aristides' adhesion to the cult of Asclepius is examined and this discussion helps us to understand the psychological reasons for Aristides performing a variety of painful divine prescriptions. In general, it is useful to take a relativistic approach for understanding what appears to the modern person as irrational behavior. From a modern psychological perspective Aristides' religiosity can be understood as a culturally constituted defense mechanism. In this context, Aristides' religiosity has a positive integrative function for his personality.

In Chapters Eight and Nine the latent contents of Aristides' dreams are examined, presenting the justification for the cross-cultural application of psychoanalysis, reasons for utilizing the conceptual tools of modern psychoanalysis, and some of the methodological problems involved. The discussion includes an identification of certain universal dream imagery in the *Sacred Tales*. Connections are also made between the manifest-content and the latent content of Aristides' dreams. Certain childhood experiences of Aristides related to child-rearing practices among the upper classes in Greco-Roman times are seen as having a causative influence in relation to the manifestation of anxiety in Aristides' dreams.

THE NATURE OF RELIGIOUS EXPERIENCE

Since this book focuses upon the religious experience of a particular individual human being, it is useful to consider the definition of the term "religious experience." Although the term "religious experience" has been used in a variety of contexts, we will define the term as the way in which human beings respond "to what is experienced as Ultimate Reality."[1] The main advantage of this definition—which was originally proposed by Joachim Wach—lies in its simplicity. Wach's definition also has applicability for the present study in that much of what is narrated in Aristides' dream diary can only be properly comprehended in the context of his relationship to his god. Many of Aristides' actions reveal an intense devotion to the god Asclepius which can only be described as an experience of "Ultimate Reality."

The value of studying the religiosity of individual human beings such as Aristides resides in the fact that it is connected to a larger project, namely, the quest for delineating the fundamental constituents of human religiosity in general. To understand religion as a human phenomenon one must study the doctrines, myths, rituals and the institutional frameworks of the multitudes of religious traditions throughout the world. However, the primary methodological presupposition of this book is that the field of religious studies also needs to explore religious phenomena as they are experienced by individuals existing within these religious traditions. In the past, the field of religious studies has placed a premium upon expanding our knowledge about the sacred myths, rituals and doctrines associated with the various religious traditions of the world. However, the working premise of this book is that more attention needs to be placed upon how these building blocks of religion are actually experienced and put in practice in the lives of religiously sensitive individuals. Such an enterprise mandates the study of the personal documents of religious individuals. In the final analysis, individual human experience is the setting for how many religious doctrines and rituals originate and continue to thrive.

---

[1] Joachim Wach, *The Comparative Study of Religion*, (New York, 1958), p. 31.

REASONS FOR THE STUDY OF INDIVIDUAL RELIGIOUS EXPERIENCE

Philosophers and historians alike have long recognized the need to study the lives of individual human beings. This need would appear to apply to the study of religious individuals as well. It was the French existential philosopher Jean Paul Sartre who applied the insights of Husserl to the study of the individual. Husserl's phenomenological method involves obtaining unbiased descriptions of objects in the world. Likewise, Sartre had an interest in conducting biographical research on individuals such as Flaubert and Genet which developed as an outgrowth of his understanding of Husserl's concept of intentionality. The concept of intentionality refers to the idea that consciousness is persistently conscious of some "object" in the world. The world of "objects" includes individual human beings as well as the cultural objects which they produce. Likewise, Wilhelm Dilthey, the nineteenth century German philosopher of history, stressed the importance of studying the concrete lives of great historical personages such as Schleiermacher and Luther. Undoubtedly, Dilthey also had an influence on Sartre's biographical method.[2]

Dilthey interpreted the individual as a microcosm existing distinctly, yet within the context of, the macrocosm of collective reality. Although human experience on the level of the individual is characterized by finitude and narrowly defined by the person's unique idiosyncrasies and psychic disposition, nevertheless the individual creates his own universe of meaning by appropriating general elements found in his social world. In respect to religious traditions of the world, each individual derives his or her personal religious beliefs based upon the religious traditions available to them in their social world and yet each individual's religiosity has a distinctive unique quality based in part upon the individual's unique psychic constitution. According to Dilthey, the individual lies at the center of historical research since the individual puts into actuality and brings to life various socio-historical structures including reli-

---

[2] Douglas Collins, *Sartre as Biographer*, (Cambridge, Mass., 1980), p. 23.

gious ideas. In this sense, the life of the individual is a mirror-image of many thematic elements of society, yet the individual can never be wholly reduced to or submerged by these cultural and social forces. In certain times of social and ideological confusion, key historical figures such as Luther and Augustine have played a significant role in the development of religious institutions. In many spheres of human activity, various "cultural heroes" have made important and sometimes catalytic contributions in the development of civilization.

Dilthey claimed that the historian is obligated to study the lives of religious, poetic, philosophical and political geniuses of history specifically by means of a careful examination of their autobiographies, letters, diaries and other personal documents. The goal of this investigative approach would be to develop a humanistic understanding of these exceptional individuals and their relationship to their society.[3] The present volume is an attempt to carefully examine the religious experience of the Greco-Roman sophist Aelius Aristides, as it is expressed in his dream diary, the *Sacred Tales*, investigating Aristides' religiosity and its description in his diary in terms of their relationship to the socio-historical world in which they existed. In other words, although Aristides represents a microcosm, we will seek to establish his relationship to the macrocosm of the Hellenistic world.

In comparison to the figures studied by Dilthey, such as Goethe and Schleiermacher, who were considered in a real sense not only to reflect general currents of the thought-world of their society, but actually to be major representatives or typical figures of that historical period, Aristides does not function as someone who dramatically re-formulated for millions of people their intellectual or theological orientation. In this sense Aristides is not a "great man of history" nor is he entirely typical in his piety. However, his diary represents an exception to the rule in that it provides rare insight into the inner life of an ancient individual. Nevertheless,

---

[3] Wilhelm Dilthey, *Selected Writings*, ed. and trans., H. P. Richman, (Cambridge, England, 1976). For a good discussion of Dilthey's ideas on individuality see Rudolf Makkreel, *Dilthey: Philosophy of the Human Studies* (Princeton, 1975), pp. 53–63.

there is no reason why students of individuality and students of religion should not turn their attention to other types of individuals besides the activist or the reformer. Of course, instead of focusing upon the process of historical change, the objective of our enterprise would be to further our understanding of the nature and dynamics of religious experience both on the individual and collective level.

Obviously, Aristides' religiosity has some connection to the social world in which he lived and in our present study we will examine the various religious, literary social and psychological forces shaping the nature of his piety. Undoubtedly, it would be fallacious to generalize about the nature of religious experience in Late Antiquity based solely upon our analysis of a single individual case. However, it would be equally wrong to maintain that Aristides' personal religion was simply too idiosyncratic or even too pathologically induced to have any significant relationship—other than one imposed by a biased historian—to certain religious currents in the Greco-Roman world.

ARISTIDES' DREAM-DIARY: THE SACRED TALES

Aristides has made available to us a vivid written account of his religious experiences while he belonged to the cult of Asclepius. This diary is entitled Οἱ Ἱεροι Λογοι or the *Sacred Tales*. However, obtaining an adequate understanding the contents of this text has posed a variety of interpretative problems for many scholars, producing a myriad of misunderstandings and contradictory interpretations. Before turning to a discussion of some of these positive and negative appraisals of the *Sacred Tales*, we will present an overview of the contents of the text as well as a brief description of the cult of Asclepius.

Aristides' spiritual diary is divided into six books which form a unique literary record of his religiously-significant dreams and waking experiences occurring over a period of seventeen years from 142 CE to the time of his death in 180 CE. During these years, Aristides was an adherent of the cult of Asclepius, a popular healing cult of the Greco-Roman world. The figure of Asclepius is first mentioned in Homer.[4] In the *Iliad*, Asclepius is described as a mortal physician whose sons Podaleirios and Machaon also practiced of the healing arts.[5] Asclepius is referred to as a "blameless physician" and a "great healer."[6] In later traditions Asclepius is worshipped as the god of medicine.[7] Once Asclepius was deified, a well-developed set of complex ritual practices grew up around him to form the cult of Asclepius. First and foremost among these rites was the practice of incubation. Individuals suffering from various physical maladies would seek divine assistance by sleeping or "incubating" at night in the temple sanctuary. The most important sanctuaries of Asclepius were located in Epidauros, Cos and Pergamum.

In classical times, Asclepius would often manifest himself directly in a patient's dream where the god would practice his healing arts upon the person. In Roman times, few persons claimed to have been healed directly by the god in their dreams. Usually, the god gave the individual in his or her dream a "divine prescription" which was performed upon waking as is exemplified by much of the material found in the *Sacred Tales*. Often, these divine prescriptions were given by the god himself without his direct presence in the dream. Frequently, these dreams were ambiguous in their meaning and required interpretation by the temple priests or by the patient himself in order to obtain the correct medical prescription. In many cases, the actual performance of many of the so-called "divine prescriptions" was quite painful. Hence, one might consider their performance to be border-line "irrational." In the case of

---

[4] The history of the cult of Asclepius is discussed by Emma and Ludwig Edelstein in *Asclepius: A Collection and Interpretation of the Testimonies, vol.II*, (New York, 1975), reprint of the 1945 edition, pp. 1–138; see also Walter Addison Jayne, *The Healing Gods of Ancient Civilizations*, (New York, 1962), pp. 240–303. Carl Kerenyi, *Asclepius*, trans. Ralph Manheim, Bollingen Series LXV, vol. III, (New York, 1959).

[5] Homer, *Iliad*, II, 732; cf. OCD s.v. "Asclepius," pp. 129–130.

[6] Iliad IV, 194; XI, 518.

[7] OCD op. cit., p. 129. The OCD reports Farnell's conclusion that the divine Asclepius has a close association with the celestial gods as opposed to the chthonic gods, in spite of the presence of certain chthonic attributes such as the snake and the incubation ritual, cf. Farnell, *Greek Hero Cults*, (Oxford, 1921).

Aristides, most of his dreams were interpreted by himself and many of the remedies of the god were agonizingly painful. On occasion, the god was known to send prophetic dreams foretelling the future to devotees such as Aristides. In general, in the Greco-Roman world the god Asclepius was known as a miracle-worker who provided salvation for humanity by means of physical healing.[8]

Although the god Asclepius is the deity who receives the most attention from Aristides once he becomes a cult-member, Asclepius is not the only god mentioned by Aristides in the *Sacred Tales* nor is he the only god worshipped by Aristides. Far from being a monotheist, Aristides was a devotee of a variety of deities found in the Greek and Egyptian pantheon. For example, S.T. Book III contains a series of visions of the Egyptian deities Sarapis and Isis. Furthermore, Aristides wrote a number of prose hymns to a variety of other gods and goddesses. Although there is no doubt that these writings present more details about Aristides' religious faith, we will focus our study upon Οι Ιεροι Λογοι, since it is there that we find the most complete expression of Aristides' religiosity.

The usual translation of the title of the diary is *Sacred Discourses*.[9] E. R. Dodds refers to the text as "Sacred Teachings" since the text is not a public address or sophistic discourse as some scholars have supposed.[10] The religious dimension of the text is underscored by the fact that the title of the text, ιεροι λογοι, was suggested by Asclepius himself. In a dream, Asclepius revealed himself to Sabinus, one of Aristides' foster-fathers, and gave his approval of Aristides' project by calling it Ιεροι Λογοι.[11]

---

[8] The Epidaurian stellae of the fourth century BCE contain numerous examples of the god operating on his patients in dreams as well as other direct methods of healing. See Edelstein, op. cit., vol. I, pp. 221–237. The subject-matter of temple medicine is discussed by Edelstein op. cit. vol. II, pp. 139–180, cf. Walter Addison Jayne, op. cit., pp. 276f.

[9] See E. R. Dodds, *Pagan and Christian in an Age of Anxiety*, (New York, 1970), p. 40, n. 3.

[10] Ibid.

[11] S.T.II.9. In this study we will rely primarily upon Behr's translation of the *Sacred Tales*. See C. A. Behr, *Aelius Aristides and the Sacred Tales*, (Amsterdam, 1968).

Depending upon the linguistic context, it is possible to translate ιεροι λογοι in three different ways, namely "sacred teachings," "sacred discourses" or "sacred tales." To call Aristides' dream book "sacred teachings" would imply that the text is a theological exposition of religious doctrines which it is not. Nor is the text a rhetorical composition which could be inferred by translating the title as "sacred discourses." If we situate the text in its proper religio-historical context, it becomes clear that primary intentions of the author in writing the text was to proclaim the fantastic revelations and miraculous healing power of Asclepius. Thus, the best translation of the term is "sacred tale" since this translation underscores the mythopoetic contents of the text.

ARISTIDES' ANCIENT BIOGRAPHERS

Excluding Aristides' own comments about his own life, there are three major ancient biographical sources dealing with the details of Aristides' life. These sources include Philostratus' *Lives of the Sophists*, the biography of Aristides recorded in the *Prolegomena*, and the *Suda* article on Aristides.[12] From these sources we learn that Aristides was a high-ranking sophist living near the city of Smyrna in Asia Minor. He was a part of the "Second Sophistic." Philostratus informs us that Aristides' father's name was Eudaemon and he was a religious official. Apparently, he was rather wealthy in that he owned a good deal of land which eventually was inherited by Aristides. Philostratus also tells us that Aristides was educated by a number of famous sophists of the day.

In regard to Aristides' sophistical skills, Philostratus states that Aristides did not like to extemporize and that he sought total precision in his work. It is noted that his rhetorical skills were employed in order to get Smyrna re-built after the town suffered a devastating earthquake. Apparently, when the emperor Marcus visited the town after the quake to survey the damage, Aristides' moving speech

---

[12] Philostratus, *Lives of the Sophists*, trans. W. Wright, Loeb Classical Library (N.Y., 1952); ed. F. Lenz, *The Aristeides Prolegomena*, treatise B, Mnemosyne, sup. 5, (Amsterdam, 1959). Suidas, *Lexicographi graeci* I, ed. Adler, p. 353f. The Suidas article is reprinted in *Aristides ex recensione Guilemi Dindorfii*, 3 vols (Leipzig, 1829).

convinced Marcus to re-build the city. As a result, a statue of Aristides was erected in his honor and he was given the title "Priest of Asclepius."

Aristides' religious interests and health issues are noted by his ancient biographers. Both Philostratus and the *Prolegomena* mention Aristides' religious diary. Philostratus incorrectly calls the text Ιερά βιβλία whereas the *Prolegomena* knows the correct title. According to Philostratus, Aristides had poor health from the time he was a boy. The phrase "a shuddering of the muscles" is used to describe his ailment.[13] Likewise, the *Prolegomena* mentions the theory that Aristides was an epileptic.[14]

Philostratus mentions that Aristides traveled abroad to Italy, Greece and Egypt. In fact, it was during one of these lengthy journeys abroad that a series of events enfolded that led to his conversion to the cult of Asclepius. Aristides himself provides us with an account of the events surrounding his conversion in Book II of his diary.

In 144 CE, at the age of twenty-four, Aristides set out on a sea voyage to Rome in the middle of winter. Once in Rome, Aristides intended to publically perform as a rhetorician for the first time. However, as fate would have it, Aristides' professional ambitions suffered an unfortunate setback. At the start of the voyage he was already sick with a cold. Paying no heed to his illness he went on to Rome anyway. By the time he arrived at the Hellespont he states that his ears were giving him trouble. Gradually his condition worsened so that he suffered from shortness of breath and a bad fever. In Rome, Aristides was unable to deliver speeches as he had originally intended and he was forced to return home.

Once at home he had his first spiritual encounter with Asclepius in a dream. Although Aristides sought out the help of the local medical doctors, these human physicians were unable to find a cure. As a result, a sort of health crisis suddenly occurred which found its resolution through Asclepius. After Aristides gave his life over to the god, the god assumed a supreme role in his life. After

---

[13] Gabrien Michenaud and Jean Dierkens, *Les Reves dans les Discours Sacres d'Aelius Aristide*, (Mons, 1972), p. 101.
[14] The *Aristeides Prolegomena*, op. cit., p. 112.

Aristides became a devotee of this cult, he was ordered by the god to keep a record his dreams. This preliminary record of his dreams forms the basic contents of the *Sacred Tales*.

ARISTIDES' MODERN BIOGRAPHERS

Ancient western religious subjectivity has been has been frequently ignored among students of Hellenistic religions, partly due to a lack of primary sources on this topic. The ancients were particularly reticent about expressing in written format their inner feelings and sentiments. These conditions have made it difficult for scholars to do much work in this area.

Such a state of affairs has not been overlooked by students of ancient religion. Campbell Bonner noted in 1937 that "classical scholars have made fruitful researches into the objective phenomena of ancient religion, particularly the Greek and Roman cults… but we still await an adequate study of the subjective side of ancient religion."[15] Martin Nilsson made a similar point when he stated that "the study of syncretism in the late antiquity has confined itself largely to the study of beliefs and doctrines but has avoided examining the spiritual soil from which these beliefs and doctrines arose."[16]

The material presented in the *Sacred Tales* represents an exception to the rule since it presents a very revealing picture of the inner life of one ancient individual. As a result, it has attracted a certain amount of attention from the scholarly community. In his 1954 Sather classical lectures entitled *Personal Religion among the Greeks*, A. J. Festugiere dedicated an entire chapter to discussing the *Sacred Tales*. Festugiere praises the *Sacred Tales* by calling it "a unique document and one of the most remarkable of antiquity."[17] E. R. Dodds made a few comments and observations on the religiosity

---

[15] Campbell Bonner, "Some Phases of Religious Feeling in Later Paganism" *Harvard Theological Review*, vol. 30, (July, 1937), p. 119.

[16] Martin Nilsson, *Geschichte der Griechischen Religion*, 2 vols. (Munchen, 1961), vol. II, p. 682cf; see also E. R. Dodds, *Pagan and Christian in an Age of Anxiety*, (New York, 1970), p. 1.

[17] A. J. Festugiere, *Personal Religion Among the Greeks*, Berkeley and Los Angeles, 1954), p. 85.

of Aristides in two seminal works *The Greeks and the Irrational* and *Pagan and Christian in an Age of Anxiety*.[18] Aristides' dreams are understood by Dodds to be psychologically authentic examples of the culture-pattern dream; that is, the structure of the dream is derived from materials culturally transmitted in the ancient world. Furthermore, Dodds states that "his dreams themselves deserve the attention of a professional psychologist, which I hope they will one day get."[19] Recently, in his 2009 book entitled *Among the Gentiles* Luke Timothy Johnson briefly discusses the *Sacred Tales* and refers to Aristides as exemplifying a particular type of religiosity which Johnson calls "participation in divine benefits."[20] In some limited sense, Aristides helps us understand the Greco-Roman religious mind set. For this reason, his piety has significance for biblical scholars. A study of Aristides' religiosity will not only further our understanding of certain popular religious trends of the era; it may also have relevance for extending our knowledge about why Christianity took root among the pagans living in the Roman world.

At this time in history, individuals throughout the ancient world were reaching out to new gods and in new ways. In the case of Aristides and other followers of the cult of Asclepius it was through the medium of the dream that contact with the numinous was achieved. For Aristides, it was in the world of his dreams where he was able to develop a spiritual relationship with Asclepius, the Greek healer god. As Patricia Cox Miller states in her study *Dreams in Late Antiquity*, for many ancients dreams served

> as one of the modes of the production of meaning… and formed a distinctive pattern of imagination which brought visual presence and tangibility to such abstract ideas as time, cosmic history, the soul and the identity of one's self. What unites this disparate material is the way

---

[18] E. R. Dodds, *The Greeks and the Irrational*, (Berkeley and Los Angeles, 1951), pp. 109–116. *Pagan and Christian in an Age of Anxiety*, op. cit. pp. 39–45.

[19] Dodds, *Pagan and Christian in an Age of Anxiety*, op. cit. p. 41.

[20] Luke Timothy Johnson, *Among the Gentiles*, (Yale University Press, 2009), pp. 51f.

in which late-antique dreamers used dreams to find meaning in their world.[21]

Upon reviewing the history of scholarship on the *Sacred Tales*, a great diversity of opinions, interpretations and assessments is apparent.[22] Depending upon their chosen field of scholarship, scholars have tended to perceive Aristides' piety through the conceptual schema of their own scholarly discipline. As a result, Aristides' religious experience has been frequently reduced in a simplistic fashion to a few fundamental concepts. For example, some psychological studies of Aristides' religiosity have reduced his piety to a product of certain unconscious psychological conflicts. Historians and students of classical rhetoric have explored the *Sacred Tales* purely from the standpoint of literary analysis and have identified various literary devices and motifs used in the text. However, the same scholars have tended to overlook the relationship between these literary motifs and the experiential dimension of the text. Thus, they have interpreted the text as a purely a rhetorical phenomenon lacking any reference to authentic religious experience.

Because of its uniqueness as an ancient religious document, there is ongoing scholarly interest in the text in various fields of the humanities including the study of religion, ancient history and the classics. For the most part, the scholarly community has treated Aristides and his religious diary in negative terms. A cursory review of the secondary literature on the text reveals two camps divided on its significance. On the one hand, scholars such as nineteenth century writers Baumgart and Konig view the *Sacred Tales* in the context of Aristides' many other rhetorical compositions. For these scholars, the *Sacred Tales* is essentially a literary composition and Aristides' religiosity as it appears in textual form is devoid of any genuine spirituality; the dreams recorded in the text are interpreted

---

[21] Patricia Cox Miller, *Dreams in Late Antiquity*, (Princeton University Press, 1994), p. 3.

[22] For a good discussion on the history of scholarship on the Sacred Tales see Michenaud and Dierkens, *Les Reves dans les "Discours Sacres" d'Aelius Aristide*, (Mons, 1971) pp. 102–104.

to be rhetorical fabrications and the product of literary invention.[23] On the other hand, another group of scholars including A. J. Festugiere, Andre Boulanger and E. R. Dodds consider the document to be a unique personal religious document, quite unlike Aristides' other rhetorical writings. For these scholars, Aristides' dream diary is a genuine religious document containing an abundance of descriptions of authentic religious experiences.

More recently, in the 2009 study entitled *Truly Beyond Wonders: Aelius Aristides and the Cult of Asclepius*, Alexis Petsalis-Diomidis has claimed that the *Sacred Tales* has "suffered from the distorting effects of 'over-realistic' readings which do not give sufficient consideration to the literary and rhetorical dimensions of the text."[24] According to Petsalis-Diomidis, Aristides writes his *Sacred Tales* for the literary purpose of constructing "a new social and intellectual elite model and he places religion at its very centre."[25] Petsalis-Diomidis believes the *Sacred Tales* is an important source of information about culture and religion in the Second Sophistic movement and yet it should be seen as a public, rhetorical composition not a private, religious diary. Previous studies of the second sophistic movement have tended to ignore the role of religion in the movement and justified such an approach by claiming that religion was not important among the elite educated classes of Roman citizens. However, religious beliefs and practices had a strong influence among the lower uneducated classes of Roman society. Although many members of the lower classes truly adhered to many of the superstitious beliefs and practices of the Greco-Roman era, religion has little relevance for understanding the culture of the elites. As a result, Aristides represented an anomaly since he belonged to the elite, educated social class of Roman citizens and was highly involved in religious activities. Therefore, to remain consistent, students of the Second Sophistic have tended to marginal-

---

[23] Konig, C. *De Aristides Incubatione*, (Jena, 1818); Baumgart, H. *Aelius Aristides als repräsentant der sophistichen rhetorikder zweitten jahrhunderts der kaiserzeit*, (Teubner, 1874).

[24] Petsalis-Diomidis, A. *Truly Beyond Wonders: Aelius Aristides and the Cult of Asclepius*, (Oxford University Press, 2009), p. 122.

[25] Ibid, p. 129.

ize Aristides and have regarded the *Sacred Tales* as an unimportant document.

Although Petsalis-Diomidis correctly states that Aristides and his *Sacred Tales* have received a disproportionately negative reaction among scholars, Aristides' piety has been dismissed for reasons other than his connection to the Second Sophistic. First, some of the marginalization of Aristides may reflect certain elements of the polemic against pagan religiosity in general which originated in the writings of the early Christian Church.[26] Second, for many modern individuals it may be difficult to take seriously Aristides' heightened attention to his body and all of the many physical ailments that plagued him throughout his life.[27] To many of us, he appears to be something of an eccentric. Third, the type of visionary religiosity expressed in the text is seen by many in the Western world as fraudulent. No doubt Aristides puzzles us. One way of dealing with him is to employ psychological jargon to label him as either "pathological," a "hypochondriac" or simply a "neurotic." Another more academic way of dismissing the genuineness of Aristides' religiosity is to claim that the *Sacred Tales* is primarily a rhetorical composition.

According to Petsalis-Diomidis, Aristides wrote the *Sacred Tales* with the goal of creating "a highly individualized, but simultaneously public model of elite religious behavior."[28] This position tends to ignore the personal religious dimension of the text and refuses to acknowledge the presence of the multitude of dreams recorded in the text. It also ignores the fact that many of the dreams recorded in the *Sacred Tales* appear to be fairly accurate descriptions of actual dream experiences.[29] It is difficult to forget this

---

[26] Johnson, 2009.

[27] Perkins, Judith, *The Suffering Self: Pain and Narrative Representation in the Early Christian Era*, (Routledge, 1995), p. 175.

[28] Petsalis-Diomidis, 2009, p. 150.

[29] Harris, William, *Dreams and Classical Antiquity*, (Harvard University Press, 2009), p. 118. Harris maintains that Aristides provides us with a fairly accurate account of his dreams. Many of the passages of the text contain strange dream-like images; there are also frequent changes in location similar to what is experienced in actual dreams. In any case, it is difficult to determine with any accuracy whether we are dealing with genuine

private dimension of spirituality expressed in the text especially when we realize that the majority of the narrative deals with religious dreams epiphanies and miraculous healings.

Petsalis-Diomidis justifies her position of seeing the text solely as a literary composition by stating that

> we are dealing with a work belonging to a well-established literary genre, that of *hieros logos*, an aetiological account of a religious activity or ceremony, or in the words of A. J. Festugiere 'an account of the apparition of a god or goddess who makes a revelation.'[30]

Furthermore, the *Sacred Tales* was grouped either by Aristides or his first editor with ten other orations and therefore it should be interpreted "in the same light as the rest of Aristides' corpus."[31] Petsalis-Diomidis states that

> although there may have been strong connections between Aristides' literary self-presentation and his public oratorical persona, and even his 'real' personality, such evidence is on the whole not available, and this discussion is focused on the textual Aristides.[32]

Likewise, she states that in the *Sacred Tales* Aristides refers to several sophists and other dignitaries mentioned in his other orations. This fact underscores the rhetorical dimension of the text and indicates that the *Sacred Tales* is primarily addressed to the sophistical community and connects the text to the process of "composition and delivery of other orations… and more generally to Aristides' career and development."[33]

Although some of the contents of the *Sacred Tales* bears witness to Aristides' familiarity with the literary conventions of his era,

---

dream narratives or simply literary embellishment. It is wrong to categorically deny the possibility the possibility of genuine dream experience being recorded in the text.

[30] Petsalis-Diomidis, p. 133.
[31] Ibid, p. 125.
[32] Ibid.
[33] Ibid, p. 126.

we should also bear in mind that the general style of the text—which can be characterized as episodic and informal—has little resemblance to the more formal literary style of other speeches. The inclusion of the *Sacred Tales* in the corpus of Aristides' rhetorical compositions is not convincing evidence that we are dealing with a public rhetorical work nor is the fact that other sophists who are referred to in Aristides' other speeches also are mentioned in the *Sacred Tales*. Since many of the dreams recorded in the text are based upon authentic dream experiences, it is unsurprising that various sophists, philosophers and other dignitaries appear in Aristides' dreams since they are frequently present in his waking life.

Petsalis-Diomidis states that the text should be interpreted as a self-conscious literary attempt to create a new elitist model of the sophist as an example of *theos aner*. Assigning Aristides the inflated status of *theos aner* is difficult to support, but Petsalis-Diomidis tries to do this by referring to the fact that Aristides mentions the process of composing the text often with the help of Asclepius. Thus, Aristides is a "divinely inspired author and suggests a high degree of self-consciousness and literary self-awareness. The very production of this text… involves divine favor."[34] Other facts are also mentioned to support her position. For example, Aristides' awareness of his own special religious status is reflected in the fact that he interpreted his own dreams rather than rely on the temple priests for this purpose. This only shows that Aristides was not unlike many others who incubated at the temple at Pergamum, Epidaurus and elsewhere. In addition, it is mentioned that Aristides was specially chosen by Asclepius and given a new name "Theodorus."[35] Again, these facts alone do not justify the somewhat grandiose conclusion that Aristides presented himself publically as an example of a *theos aner*. Alleging that one received divine inspiration as part of the writing process does not necessarily equate with viewing oneself or inviting others to see oneself as a charismatic prophet. A close reading of the text reveals that Aristides' self-understanding precludes such awareness on his part. Aristides was not enamored of his religious experiences to the point of seeing

---

[34] Ibid.
[35] S.T.IV.51–52.

himself as a charismatic prophet in the same sense as many did in the third and fourth century CE. As Peter Brown notes, the concept of *theos aner* is a far more developed institutional role in the third and fourth century when credulity was at its highest.[36] Nevertheless, compared to Aristides' rhetorical ambition, the expression of genuine religious sentiments is decidedly a more significant element in the *Sacred Tales*. More to the point, the text presents a detailed picture of religious feelings surrounding Aristides' involvement in the cult of Asclepius, not the fulfillment of Aristides' professional ambitions as a sophist.

The religious and psychological dimensions of the text have not gone unnoticed by various scholars and not all of the attention has been of a negative nature. From the negative standpoint, Campbell Bonner calls Aristides "a brain-sick noodle."[37] On the other hand, others such as A. J. Festugiere, and more recently, Luke Timothy Johnson view the text in a more positive light. In general, these scholars accept the genuineness of Aristides' religiosity. For Festugiere, Aristides' religiosity probably did not seem very unusual or different to his peers, especially among the more credulous members of the Roman upper class. According to Timothy Luke Johnson, Aristides' piety is an example of "participation in divine benefits" and to some extent even typifies some of the spiritual sentiments of the time.[38] From the point of view of students of early Christianity, Aristides may give us insight into the Greco-Roman religious world into which early Christianity spread during the first and second century CE.

Perhaps, no one does a better job at marginalizing Aristides than E. R. Dodds who briefly refers to Aristides in his two often-cited works *The Greeks and the Irrational* and *Pagan and Christian in an Age of Anxiety*.[39] As Robert Smith points out "the great merit of E.

---

[36] Brown, Peter, *The Making of Late Antiquity*, (Cambridge University Press, 1972) pp. 41–44.

[37] Bonner, Campbell, "Some Phases of Religious Feeling in Later Paganism," *Harvard Theological Review*, vol. 30, n. 3, p. 125.

[38] Johnson, p. 51; Festugiere, p. 85.

[39] Dodds, E. R. *Pagan and Christian in an Age of Anxiety*, p. 39–45; *The Greeks and the Irrational*, pp. 109–116.

R. Dodds' study *Pagan and Christian in an Age of Anxiety*, 1965 is that it employs psychological explanations to cast new light on the religious experience of late antiquity."[40] Dodds selected certain religious figures such as Aristides, St. Perpetua and Marcus Aurelius who exemplify some of the new spiritual trends of what Dodds calls the "age of anxiety." One of the central characteristics of the "age of anxiety" is what Robert Smith describes as a contempt on the part of both pagans and Christians alike "for the human condition and hatred of the body."[41]

In discussing Aristides and the *Sacred Tales*, Dodds places emphasis upon a discussion of Aristides' anxiety dreams, which are seen by Dodds as examples of the culture pattern dream, and Aristides' performance of various painful divine prescriptions, which are viewed by Dodds as examples of pathological behavior. In concentrating our attention on these two phenomena, Dodds constructs his argument that Aristides typifies some of the major socio-historical trends of "the age of anxiety." Accordingly, Aristides and many of his fellow contemporaries involved in the quest for salvation whether it be through receiving a direct revelation from the gods in a dream or through initiation were acting out a certain kind of behavior described as "the fear of freedom—the unconscious flight from the heavy burden of individual choice which an open society lays upon its members."[42] Dodds accepts Aristides' dream accounts as psychologically authentic examples of the "culture-pattern dream" and he is willing to portray Aristides as a genuine religious individual. However, he tends to misconstrue the nature of Aristides' piety by attaching the "anxious pagan" label to Aristides. Robert Smith extends Dodds' ideas further by stating that "Aristides was a 'sick soul' living in a time when his contempo-

---

[40] Smith, R. "Misery and Mystery: Aelius Aristides" in *Pagan and Christian Anxiety*, ed. R. Smith and J. Lounibus, (Lanham, MD, 1984), p. 29.

[41] Smith, R. Ibid.

[42] Dodds, E. R., 1970, p. 252. There are others who have applied the label "anxious pagan" to Aristides. Cf. Reardon, B., "The Anxious Pagan," May 12th edition, Ontario Classical Association: Trent University, pp. 81–93.

raries like Marcus Aurelius began to see life with new perceptions."[43]

Undoubtedly Aristides may have had certain psychological problems which may have affected his religious as well as non-religious behavior. However, it is a mistake to label his entire religious life as a symptom of his neurosis. The first and second centuries CE saw a dramatic shift in the spiritual landscape of the Greco-Roman world characterized by a new collective interest in personal salvation, the occult and the eastern religious beliefs and practices. Aristides' religiosity to a certain degree reflects many of these same religious and cultural trends present in his era. However, we question the validity of using the notion of personal and/or collective anxiety or the "fear of freedom" as the complete answer for understanding the motivations of Aristides and others like him. Undoubtedly, there are purely religious motivations as well and these religious considerations are poorly served by labeling Aristides a "sick soul" or an "anxious pagan." Our argument may also hold for others in Greco-Roman society besides Aristides. However, in this book we will restrict our comments to Aristides; we are willing to admit that some of our conclusions may have a more general applicability to others as well living in Late Antiquity.

Aristides and his dream diary have not always received fair treatment in the scholarly literature. In a simplistic attempt to explain away Aristides' type of religiosity, the *Sacred Tales* has been misinterpreted either as a product of literary invention or his personality has been branded as either "narcissistic," "pathological," or "neurotic." Another more inventive way of describing him is to call him a "sick soul" or simply "the anxious pagan." Upon situating this dream diary and its author in the proper religio-historical context, that is, in the context of ancient Mediterranean religious traditions, it becomes clear that Aristides may have had certain psychological struggles but he does not deserve to be labeled an "anxious pagan." Instead, he is a particularly unique example of *homo religiosus*. Anxiety may have had its effects upon Aristides' religion but it does not wholly define it. Given the fact that Aristides was a fully functioning sophist, a respected member of his community and a

---

[43] Smith, R. Ibid p. 48.

deeply religious individual, it makes more sense to label Aristides as the "not-so-anxious pagan."

METHODOLOGICAL QUESTIONS

Rather than understanding the text from one scholarly perspective, this book brings together insights from various disciplines: the historical sciences as well as social sciences including both the field of psychology and anthropology in order to consider the text from a variety of perspectives. The phenomenon of religion is the embodiment of a complex set of doctrines, myths, rituals, institutions, and experiences all of which are intertwined together.[44] When interpreting the contents of a particular individual's religious experience such as Aristides, an interdisciplinary approach in the study of religion will allow us to perceive each of the strands of religion reflected in an individual's religious behavior.

The existence of Aristides' dream diary poses some interesting scholarly questions which have not been fully answered. For example, are the dreams recorded in this diary based upon actual genuine dream experiences or are they merely the product of literary invention? To what extent does the text contain accurate descriptions of actual dream experiences and to what extent are we dealing with purely fictitious literary creations? Will we ever be able to provide an adequate answer to this question? What methods and procedures can we employ to determine an answer to this question? If so, what are they? Are there any reliable criteria that we can establish that would enable us to determine the authenticity of these dreams? Can we identify any literary conventions and motifs present in the text and can we explain what their relationship is to the experiential dimension of the text?

If indeed the dreams recorded in the *Sacred Tales* are authentic in the sense that they are genuine descriptions of Aristides' dream experiences, then we can utilize the methods of modern dream researchers including the work done by Freudian psychoanalysis to

---

[44] For a cogent description of the interdisciplinary approach in the study of religion see Ninian Smart's *The Science of Religion and the Sociology of Knowledge*, (Princeton University Press, 1973).

shed light on the meaning of his dreams and the religious piety recorded in the text.

Of course other questions remain to be answered as well. One important issue regarding Aristides and his dreams has to do with the issue about the extent to which he is a representative figure or merely an eccentric. To what extent does the case of Aristides help to inform us about the social and religious trends of the era? To what degree does Aristides have relevance for the understanding of the religious climate of Late Antiquity or is he simply too eccentric to have any relevance? These questions need to be addressed.

Our employment of the tools of modern psychology and psychoanalysis implies that we are willing to consider certain aspects of Aristides' psyche which go beyond the realm of conscious experience. In other words, when we examine Aristides' dreams and the symbolism associated with them, our interpretation of them may lead us into the realm of the unconscious. One of the drawbacks of a purely phenomenological method as it is articulated in the writings of Dilthey, Sartre and Husserl is that it fails to examine particular elements of an individual psyche that the individual may not be consciously aware of.[45] Hence, there is a need to complement our phenomenological description of Aristides' religious experience with the methods of explanatory psychology. Given that Aristides offers a fairly uncensored account of his dreams, he is an ideal subject for analysis.

Similar work has been done. In the psychobiography of Martin Luther entitled *Young Man Luther*, 1958, Erik Erikson combined the methods and concepts of two academic disciplines, namely, history and psychoanalysis to create the new field of psychohistory.[46] Erikson shared Dilthey's interest in studying "cultural workers" and employed a biographical method in an attempt to map out

---

[45] Joseph Havens, "The Participant's vs. the Observer's Frame of Reference in the Psychological Study of Religion," *Journal of the Scientific Study of Religion*, vol. 1, (Oct. 1961), p. 83.

[46] Erik Erikson *Young Man Luther: A Study in Psychoanalysis and History*, (New York, 1958); see also *Gandhi's Truth*, (New York, 1968); for more information on psychohistory see *Explorations in Psychohistory*, ed. Robert J. Lifton, (New York, 1975).

the dynamic relationship existing between the individual and his social and historical environment. Unlike Dilthey, Erikson is a spokesperson for Freudian psychoanalysis which implies his acceptance of Freud's concept of the unconscious and theory of the instincts into his work. Rather than operating purely on the plane of consciousness, Erikson's psycho-historical investigations often lead the reader into the realm of unconscious impulses, the libido and the Oedipus complex. In keeping with Erikson's ideas, towards the end of our study of Aristides we will incorporate many of the insights of modern psychoanalysis into our analysis of the religiosity of Aristides.

Chapter Two: The Literary Dimension of the Text

Aristides: An Example of Homo Religiosus

This chapter demonstrates that the *Sacred Tales* should be regarded as first and foremost a personal religious document and that Aristides exhibits the fundamental characteristics of a highly religious person. Before elucidating the positive dimension of Aristides' religiosity and pointing out some of the shortcomings of portraying him as an "anxious pagan" or a "sick soul," we need to explain why the *Sacred Tales* is a good example of a personal religious document as opposed to a public rhetorical document. The *Sacred Tales* reveals to us another side of Aristides besides Aristides the sophist. In addition to being a gifted sophist, Aristides' personal religious experience is highlighted in the *Sacred Tales*. By stating this, we do not however wish to imply that Aristides self-consciously assumed the institutional role of *theos aner*.

Fundamental to our argument is the notion that Aristides' religiosity was authentic and it served a positive psychological function. To argue such a position, we must evaluate Aristides' religious experience as it appears in the text. This does not involve proving the veracity or falsehood of the multitude of supernatural events recorded in the *Sacred Tales*. Naturally, as a modern person living in the scientific age, it may be difficult for us to accept the concrete reality of divine epiphanies or "appearances of the god" within the dreams of ancient individuals such as Aristides. Similarly, it may appear to the reader that we are naively accepting the reality of the various divine healings reported in the *Sacred Tales*. This issue raises some interesting questions about the proper methods needed to study the religious experiences of others belonging to various religious traditions of the world.

When approaching religious doctrines and practices which are quite different from our own, there may be a temptation to dismiss those foreign spiritual ideas and practices as false on the grounds that they are simply too strange to be taken seriously. However, to develop an empathetic and accurate descriptive analysis of those beliefs and practices, it is necessary for the student of religion to bracket his or her metaphysical and epistemological assumptions regarding this material. Our interest is not to validate or to disprove these ideas but simply to understand them from the standpoint of the believer.

Hence, the first guiding principle of this investigation is that we must accept the fact that from the standpoint of the phenomenology of religion, the dream-revelation is an authentic expression of the religious consciousness. In fact, phenomena such as religious visions, dream-oracles and other states of ecstasy are a familiar part of the history of religions, occurring in a wide variety of cultural and historical contexts, including the religious traditions of primitive peoples as well as the religions of the ancient west. In this sense, all the dreams recorded by Aristides in the *Sacred Tales* have spiritual significance. Further, we shall see that certain aspects of Aristides' religiosity display the universal features the religious life, especially his interest in salvation in the form of physical well-being, his vision-quest and his intense devotion and love of his god. From the perspective of methodology, the student of religion is obligated to accept the autonomy of religion.

The second guiding principle is that religious experience is always communicated to others through a particular medium such as symbolism, myth, theological doctrines or, in Aristides' case, religious autobiography. As Joaquin Wach states, "like all kinds of experience, religious experience tends to expression."[1] Furthermore, Wach notes some of the reasons why religious individuals desire to communicate to others the nature of their religious experience. First, the experience of the divine has an explosive quality producing in individuals the need to "give vent to joy and pain."[2] Second,

---

[1] Wach, op. cit., p. 59.
[2] Ibid, p. 60.

there is a desire to share with others the "awesome nature of what has been experienced."³

The third guiding principle for this study is that there is a propagandistic tendency to "attract and invite others to see and hear as one has seen and heard."⁴ The available forms of religious expression vary according to the historical and cultural circumstances in which individuals find themselves. In the case of Aristides, his religious experience found its literary expression in the form of a dream diary. Many of the characteristics of this diary conform to the fundamental constituents of the literary category known as *aretalogy*. Chapter Four considers in further detail how the *Sacred Tales* exhibits some of the characteristics of aretalogy, but for now it is worth mentioning that although the *Sacred Tales* is quite unique in that it is the only "dream diary" extant from ancient times, there are several other religious documents originating in the same era which contain descriptions of dream epiphanies, visions and miraculous healings. Later in this Chapter, we will identify some of these texts and discuss some of their contents in comparison to the *Sacred Tales*, situating the *Sacred Tales* in the context of other visionary writings originating in the ancient Western religious tradition and determining to what extent we are dealing with genuine religious experience.

THE SACRED TALES AND ANCIENT AUTOBIOGRAPHY

Part of the problem with adequately comprehending the religious experience of Aristides and others like him is that we will never be able to know his experience directly. We can only access his experience through a text. As a literary text, Aristides' diary presents an account of his dreams and it also includes a description of several types of supernatural occurrences. From the standpoint of the religious believer, his dreams were sacred revelations, as opposed to illusory psychological creations of a deluded mind. Thus, the text represents the literary means by which Aristides was able to describe his inner psychological experiences, the meaning of which is

---

³ Ibid., pp. 232–233.
⁴ Ibid.

primarily fixed in his apprehension of Asclepius in his dreams as well as the appearance of "divine messages" communicated symbolically to him in his dreams.

Given such factors, Aristides never desired to share with others the chronological story of his life. He did not possess the same literary aspirations in composing his diary as the aspirations of a modern autobiographer. Unlike modern autobiographical accounts, the *Sacred Tales* could never be described as "life-history" in which the autobiographer tells the story of his or her life in chronological order. Concerns such as these are traditionally associated with the literary intentions of the modern autobiographer. The main thrust of Aristides' narrative is of a theological nature, that is, Aristides' theological viewpoint colors the way in which he narrates the material presented in the text. If we were attempting to locate Aristides' motivation for writing his diary, we would have to settle on religious factors as having the most important role. The faith-commitment of Aristides tends to function as the central guiding principle for understanding the miracles and other supernatural phenomena discussed in the text.

In terms of its historicity, the text incorporates "factual" data about Aristides' life such as the information that he was a resident of the temple at Pergamum or that his servant Zosimus was his close friend. However, this "objective-historical" dimension of the text can be easily distinguished from the religious dimension of the text. Obviously, the religio-historical phenomena described in the text step outside the boundaries of scientific fact. It is important to remember that much of the contents of the text consist of "religious data." When approaching this material we need to remember that the text was written by a highly enthusiastic believer and therefore the text reflects the theological beliefs and values of its author.

In composing the *Sacred Tales*, it is rather obvious that in some measure Aristides' raw dream experiences have been given structure and embellishment in the process of their expression in a literary document. We do not mean to imply that Aristides set out to intentionally falsify the facts. Instead, it merely means that the process of secondary elaboration was involved in the recording of his dreams. Secondary elaboration occurs as time passes by and the conscious mind tends to alter the details of the original dream experience when it tries to recall them. Unfortunately, we will never have access to Aristides' original dream experience, only that which has been filtered by Aristides' conscious mind. Aristides was the recipient of a type of dream-experience which was consciously interpreted by him and those belonging to the cult of Asclepius as "religious." Dream epiphanies such as those recorded by Aristides were accepted as part of the cultural imagination of ancients and so it is not out of the ordinary that an individual such as Aristides made claims of having such experiences.[5]

Although the term "religious experience" tends to connote an inner psychological dimension of human experience, we should not forget that any personal religious experience, including those had by Aristides, can be understood as such because that type of experience was identified as religious by the religious traditions of that era. In short, we should avoid seeing Aristides' dream-visions as being completely detached and autonomous from his cultural environment, as if one could artificially remove "pure experience" from its linguistic and cultural context. Aristides' visionary experiences reflect many of the religious doctrines and beliefs present in the cult of Asclepius.

Furthermore, Aristides was not only a religious devotee. He was also an orator and Aristides employs the tools of his oratorical trade to give expression to the details of his experiences in the cult of Asclepius. As Laurent Pernot correctly notes, Aristides is an example of "the orator as a religious figure."[6] This does not necessarily imply that the *Sacred Tales* is wholly a rhetorical composition and nothing more. However, much of the vocabulary and the literary techniques Aristides uses for describing his dreams have strong similarities and parallels to the language and literary motifs found in other ancient dream accounts.

As we have stated, the *Sacred Tales* is not a chronological account of its author' life. In writing the *Sacred Tales,* Aristides does not spend any time discussing his childhood, his youth, growing

---

[5] For a discussion about the relationship between religious doctrine and religious experience including mystical experiences, see Peter Moore, "Mystical Experience, Mystical Doctrine, Mystical Technique" in *Mysticism and Philosophical Analysis*, ed. Steven Katz, (New York, 1978).

[6] Laurent Pernot, "The Rhetoric of Religion," *Rhetorica*, Vol. 24, issue 3, pp. 235–254.

up, and so forth. Rather than presenting his life in chronological order he concentrates upon one aspect of his life, to be sure, the quintessential element of his life, namely, his spiritual bond to Asclepius. Although several other people are mentioned—such as his foster father Epagathus as well as various servants, civic officials, orators and friends—there is no doubt that the main characters of the narrative are Aristides and Asclepius. Although "objective" factual information is presented, the main focus of the text is of a religious nature.

Although our main concern is with spiritual documents originating from the ancient West, it is worth noting that in the Greco-Roman tradition many secular writers occasionally wrote about themselves and they did so by using a variety of literary forms, including the epistle, the rhetorical treatise, poetry, as well as philosophical writings. The literary genre of autobiography, however, did not exist as a distinct type of writing. Of course, this state of affairs does not imply that the ancients did not write about themselves in various ways. In fact, there are numerous types of ancient documents which display an autobiographical aspect in spite of the fact that the generic distinction was not made.[7] The word "autobiography" itself is a modern invention: the word does not appear in ancient literature. Momigliano informs us that according to the O.E.D. the word was first used in 1809 by Robert Southey.[8] The 1866 edition of the Grand Dictionnaire Universal Larousse states that the word "autobiography" was first used in the English language.[9]

Perhaps the best modern study of ancient autobiography was written by a student of Wilhelm Dilthey named Georg Misch. In his monumental two-volume study entitled *A History of Autobiography in Antiquity*, Misch traces the emergence of subjectivity and individuality in ancient times.[10] According to Misch, there are only

---

[7] Elizabeth Bruss, *Autobiographical Acts*, (Baltimore, 1976), ch. 1.

[8] See Arnoldo Momigliano, *The Development of Greek Biography*, (Cambridge, Mass., 1971), p. 14.

[9] Momigliano, Ibid.

[10] George Misch, *A History of Autobiography in Antiquity*, 3rd ed.; 2 vols, (Cambridge, Mass., 1951).

nine complete autobiographies prior to the *Confessions* of St. Augustine. These texts are listed as *Brutus* by Cicero, 46 BCE, *On His Own Life and Education* by Nicolaus Damascenus, 10 CE, *Tristia IV.10*, by Ovid, 10 CE, the *Res Gestae* of Augustus, 14 CE, *Life* by Josephus, CE, *The Dream* by Lucian, 165 CE, the *Sacred Tales* by Aelius Aristides, 171 CE, the *Meditations* by Marcus Aurelius, 180 CE and lastly, Gregorius Thaumaturgus' address of thanks to Origen, 239 CE. In addition, autobiographical reflections can also be found in other ancient writings including the *Metamorphoses* Book XI, the poetry of Hesiod and Archilochus as well as Plato's Seventh Letter and the Epistles of Paul. Misch's real interest is not to study "autobiography" *per se*. Instead, his goal is to examine the early history of self-awareness. In respect to the *Sacred Tales*, Misch points out that it has a "strangely modern" aspect to it since Aristides spends an inordinate amount of time discussing his religious sentiments and reflecting upon his responses to his visionary experiences.[11] Momigliano states that often ancient writers wrote about themselves in an objective way, recounting facts, events, and concrete data as opposed to feelings.[12]

It is perhaps due to the fact that personal spiritual documents were so rare in antiquity that the spiritual and personal flavor of the *Sacred Tales* was virtually overlooked by Philostratus. In his *Lives of the Sophists*, Philostratus refers to the *Sacred Tales* merely as a work of rhetorical art.[13] The word εφημερίδες meaning "diaries" or "daybooks" is used by Philostratus in reference to the *Sacred Tales*. Philostratus may be referring to S.T.I.4–61 which consists of a day-to-day account illnesses and treatment. It is also possible that Philostratus only knew about the first book of the *Sacred Tales* which would explain why he referred to it as "day-books."[14] On the other hand, based upon his comments on the *Sacred Tales*, Synesius

---

[11] Misch, op. cit., vol. 2, p. 508.

[12] Momigliano, ibid, p. 15.

[13] Philostratus, op. cit., p. 214.

[14] See H. Baumgart, *Aelius Aristide Als Repräsentant Der Sophistischen Rhetorik der zweiten Jahrhundrerts Der Kaiserzeit*, (Leipzig, 1974) p. 65, n. 63. Cf. Nicolai Rudolph, *Gesch. Der Gesammt. Griech. Literatur*, (Magdeburg, 1865), p. 398.

was probably familiar with the entire text. His comments regarding Philostratus' discussion is revealing. The oneirocritically-minded Synesius states that although day-books are a suitable format for every kind of oratory regardless of how trivial it might be, "night books" such as Aristides' diary should be reserved for only very important rhetorical topics.[15]

In his nineteenth-century study of the *Sacred Tales*, Baumgart cites these passages written by Philostratus and Synesius in order to make the following point: since both Philostratus and Synesius regard the text as primarily a rhetorical composition, it does not make any sense for modern scholars such as Welcher to claim that the text possesses any spiritual profundity or depth. This, of course, is a fallacious argument. Baumgart points out that neither Philostratus nor Synesius made any reference to Aristides' deep religious sentiment. In fact, Baumgart found it difficult to locate any authentic autobiographical impulse in the text. According to Baumgart, this implies that Aristides was a dishonest narrator of his experiences in the cult of Asclepius and he rejects the notion that the text contains anything of interest to the historian or psychologist of religion. First and foremost, Aristides was a sophist and sophists were often known to blur the distinction between truth and fiction in the telling of their entertaining tales. In Baumgart's view, Aristides' primary objective in writing the *Sacred Tales* was to compose an entertaining rhetorical work, without necessarily telling the truth about his life.[16]

In contrast to Baumgart's nineteenth-century point-of-view, William Harris has recently taken the opposite perspective. In his study of ancient dreams entitled *Dreams and Experience in Classical Antiquity*, Harris states that in spite of his egotism, Aristides "emerges as a rare and relatively convincing informant."[17] Based upon his analysis of Aristides' dreams, Harris concludes that in comparison to other ancient dream accounts Aristides' dreams are

---

[15] *The Letters of Synesius of Cyrene*, trans. Augustine Fitzgerald, (London, 1926), p. 355.

[16] Baumgart, op. cit., p. 103.

[17] William Harris, *Dreams and Experience in Classical Antiquity*, (Harvard University Press, 2009), p. 118.

for the most part genuine.¹⁸ His conclusion is based upon the following fact: there is a preponderance of strange dream-like images in many of Aristides' dream-reports; the dream-like quality to the narrative is characterized by frequent, unexplained changes in locations. For the purposes of our study we shall assume that unless there is some other reason to the contrary we shall take the view that Harris is correct in his conclusion; we will regard the material recorded in the text as an accurate description what Aristides actually dreamt, although we are willing to admit that there may be a certain degree of secondary elaboration or distortion in certain cases.

ANCIENT VISIONARY LITERATURE

Aristides was not the only person in ancient times who wrote an account about personal encounters with the divine. Several other ancient Greco-Roman religious texts provide first-person narratives involving contact with the gods. For example, in a letter addressed to Caesar Augustus, a first century CE doctor named Thessalos of Tralles discusses his vision of Asclepius.¹⁹

Thessalos' letter presents an account of his search for religious truth and this quest takes him on a journey throughout Asia Minor and Egypt. Finally, after travelling far and wide throughout the ancient world, Thessalos reaches the breaking point. Stretching his arms out into the air, he asks the gods for some kind of vision that would permit him to end his quest and return home in Alexandria. After this episode, Thesallos meets an elderly priest who agrees to assist Thessalos in his quest to obtain a religious revelation. First, both Thessalos and the priest fast for three days. Then, the priest gives Thessalos a choice. Thesallos can either receive a vision of a spirit or a vision of a god. Thessalos chooses to see a god. After this Thessalos is led to a house where he has a vision of Asclepius

---

¹⁸ Ibid.
¹⁹ *Catalogus Codicum Astrologonum Graecorum VIII* (Cod. Parisinon) 3; see Festugiere, A. "L'Experience Religieuse Du Medecin Thessalos," *Revue Biblique*, vol. 48 (1939), pp. 45–77. Cf. Festugiere, *La Revelation D'Hermes Trismegiste*, 2 vols., (Paris, 1950), vol. I, pp. 56–58.

and during the vision Asclepius and Thessalos engage in a dialogue concerning medicinal plants.

In commenting upon the letter and other literary evidence like it, A. D. Nock states that "such a religious quest was no doubt a real experience... The most authoritative guidance comes direct from the gods as to Nechepso or Thessalos or the writer of the Revelation of Hermas or the Katochoi; ecstasy is another way."[20] A. J. Festugiere is of the opinion that figures such as Thessalos and Aristides truly believed that they were seeing the gods and that their personal narratives take us beyond the realm of the purely literary.[21]

Another piece of evidence is found in an inscription from the temple of Mandulis at the town of Talmis in Nubia.[22] In the inscription it states,

> I had a vision and found rest for my soul. For thou didst grant my prayer and show me thyself going through the heavenly vault; then washing thyself in the holy water of immortality thou appeared again. Thou didst come at due season to thy shrine, making thy rising, and giving to thy image and to thy shrine divine breath and great power.[23]

Dreams and visions are mentioned in ancient Christian literature as well. For example, four dreams of St. Perpetua and a vision of Satyrus are recorded in the text *The Martyrdom of Saints Perpetua and Felicitas*.[24]

Perpetua was a Christian martyr who lived in North Africa towards the end of the second century CE. While she was incarcerated in the city of Carthage awaiting her execution, Perpetua received four dream-visions which she wrote down. In the first

---

[20] A. D. Nock, *Conversion*, (Oxford, 1952), p. 110.

[21] Festugiere, "L'Experience Religieuse Du Medicin Thessalos," op. cit., p. 73.

[22] A. D. Nock, "A Vision of Mandulis Aion," *Harvard Theological Review*, vol. 27, (1934), pp. 53–104.

[23] Nock, "A Vision of Mandulis Aion," op. cit. p. 64.

[24] Trans. Herbert Musurillo, *The Acts of the Christian Martyrs*, (London, 1972), pp. 106–131.

dream vision, Perpetua sees a large ladder made of brass extending up into heaven. Attached to the ladder are a number of different sharp objects such as blades and spikes. A huge dragon was at the bottom of the ladder. Satyrus was the first to climb up the ladder, followed by Perpetua. Satyrus warns Perpetua about the dragon and once she climbs the ladder, she enters into a heavenly garden where she encounters a tall white-haired old man who offers her a piece of cheese which Perpetua eats. In the second dream-vision Perpetua sees her deceased brother Dinocrates who is very thirsty. On his face is the cancerous wound which had caused his death. Standing by a water-basin, Dinocrates is unhappy because he is unable to reach the edge of the basin. However, in the third dream-vision Dinocrates is now able to reach the water basin and his face is clean. The facial wound is now gone. At the side of the basin is a golden flask with water in it. Regardless of how much Dinocrates drinks from the flask, it mysteriously remains full. In the fourth and last dream-vision Perpetua is led to a great arena where she engages in a fierce battle with a gigantic Egyptian warrior. While preparing for the fight, Perpetua is transformed into a man. Once the battle ensues, Perpetua is triumphant, the crowd cheers her victory and her dream ends.

These four dream-visions of Perpetua differ from the visions of Aristides and Thessalos since in the former case there are no dream epiphanies. However, in Perpetua's first dream we encounter an old man who can be interpreted symbolically as a heavenly shepherd. Likewise, the evil Egyptian in the fourth dream could be taken to represent the devil, as Dodds thinks.[25] If we examine the dream images recorded in this text, most of the material is very dream-like and bears a strong resemblance to the typical features of actual dreams. Hence, it is difficult to conclude the material is not genuine. This conclusion is reinforced by the fact that Perpetua does not record any miraculous or supernatural events, unlike Aristides. In distinction to Perpetua's dreams, the vision of Satyrus, which follows in chapters eleven through thirteen, incorporates an abundance of stereotypical Christian symbols and images such as "angels carrying off the soul, other still greater angels of the Pres-

---

[25] E. R. Dodds, *Pagan and Christian in an Age of Anxiety*, op. cit. p. 51.

ence, walls of light, voices crying 'Holy, Holy, Holy,' elders arranged in a neat row on either side of the throne."[26] For these reasons, Dodds comes to the conclusion that the vision of Satyrus has little psychological authenticity.[27]

Other instances of visionary experiences can be cited in ancient Western religious literature. For example, in the Old Testament there are numerous visionary accounts which in turn have influenced New Testament writers. For example, the book of Daniel records six stories and four dream-visions. Similar accounts appear in the book of *Enoch* and Syriac *Baruch* as well as in the book of Revelation in the New Testament. Thus in *I Enoch* 14:8 we read,

> [T]he vision was shown to me this: Behold, in the vision clouds invited me and a mist summoned me, and the course of the stars and the lightnings sped and hastened me, and the winds in the vision caused me to fly and lifted me upward and bore me into heaven.[28]

The Shepherd of Hermas is an important Christian example of ancient visionary literature. In the *Gospel of Peter* we read,

> [N]ow in the night whereon the Lord's day dawned, as the soldiers were keeping guard two by two in every watch, there came a great sound in the heaven and they saw the heavens opened and two men descend thence, shining with a great light, and drawing near unto the sepulcher.[29]

Because this particular account is so heavily imbued with Christian theological images, we probably are dealing with a literary device as opposed to actual experiences. However, this is not always the

---

[26] Dodds, *Pagan and Christian in an Age of Anxiety*, op. cit., p. 49.

[27] Ibid.

[28] See also Ezek 3:14; 8:3. On the problem of determining the psychological authenticity of such accounts see Geo. Widengren, *Literary and Psychological Aspects of the Hebrew Prophets*, (Uppsala, 1948) pp. 94–123.

[29] *Gospel of Peter*, IX 35–36, *The Apocryphal New Testament*, trans. James Montague, (London, 1927), p. 92.

case, as in *The Visions of Zosimus*, an alchemical text roughly from the same era.[30]

Zosimus of Panopolis lived in the third century CE. In the text's first dream-vision, Zosimus sees a sacrificer standing on an altar. Another figure named Ion, the priest of the inner sanctuaries, tells Zosimus about the painful process of his metamorphosis from the flesh into the spirit. Upon seeing the "mutilated anthroparian" spewing forth his own flesh, Zosimus is frightened into consciousness and the dream ends. In the other dream-visions, there is vivid imagery, much of which has alchemical associations yet there is no reason to believe that these dream-visions are purely the product of literary invention. In C. G. Jung's opinion,

> [I]ts salient features seem to indicate that for Zosimus it was a highly significant experience which he wished to communicate to others. Although alchemical literature contains a number of allegories, which without doubt are merely didactic fables and are not based on direct experience, the vision of Zosimus may well have been an actual experience.[31]

Based upon our brief review of ancient visionary literature, it appears that Aristides' dream-diary is not entirely unique in ancient times in terms of its subject matter. Nor can we categorically deny the possibility that such accounts contain descriptions of actual psychological experiences. Religious visions, including both those of the waking and sleeping variety, were recorded and treated in textual form in a variety of ancient religious contexts including ancient Egyptian religion, ancient Judaism, Christianity, and Greco-Roman religion, including the cult of Asclepius.

As students of religion, our task is not to determine the truth or falsity of the religious beliefs, practices, or experiences described by the adherents of the various religious traditions under consideration. Hence, we must bracket our metaphysical assumptions concerning the genuineness of the religious experiences described in

---

[30] "The Visions of Zosimus" in C.G. Jung's *Alchemical Studies*, Bollingen Series XX, (Princeton, 1967), pp. 59–109.

[31] Jung, op. cit., p. 66.

these texts. It is a methodological error to say that that the authors of these writings simply made up stories about their visions of the gods, dream epiphanies and other supernatural events recorded in these texts. A corollary to this point is that if we doubt the authenticity of the dreams of Aristides along with the visions of Perpetua and others like them, then there would be no reason to analyze Aristides' dreams or the visions of Perpetua from a psychological perspective. If the texts do not contain actual religious dreams or visions but rather literary fictions, then such material should be addressed purely as a literary phenomenon. On the contrary, if we take an empathetic look at Aristides and his religious diary, what we find is a genuinely religious individual whose dream visions provide us with insight into many of the characteristics of Hellenistic personal religion.

The strength of this position is reinforced by a couple of considerations. Aristides' religiosity bears similarities to the characteristics of other spiritual individuals throughout history. One essential feature of the religious consciousness is an awareness of ineffability in the presence of the divine. Aristides' religious experience displays the quality of ineffability and the sense of wonder and awe in the presence of the holy. If we reject the genuineness of his religiosity, then we might as well reject the genuineness of all religious experience in general. If we narrow our focus to Greco-Roman times, Aristides' piety is especially comparable, although in a somewhat exaggerated form, to the religious behavior of many of his peers in the cult of Asclepius as well as other popular cults of the day. This fact alone underscores the religious dimension of Aristides' behavior and personality. Most of Aristides' dreams appear to be genuine psychological experiences in the sense that they are filled with surrealistic imagery; Aristides' accounts of these dreams contain dreamlike language. For these reasons it makes sense for us to accept the text on its own terms as a religious document; in other words, our understanding of Aristides' religious dream diary is increased if we approach it with a sense of respect and empathy for its contents.

CHAPTER THREE: THE PROBLEM OF INDIVIDUALITY IN THE SACRED TALES: COMPARING THE SACRED TALES WITH OTHER SELECTED ANCIENT CHRISTIAN AND PAGAN AUTOBIOGRAPHICAL DOCUMENTS

ARISTIDES, THE HEALTHY-MINDED VERSUS ST. AUGUSTINE, THE SICK SOUL

This chapter draws comparisons between the *Sacred Tales* and a few other ancient religious autobiographies. First, we will turn to Christian writings and compare the *Sacred Tales* to a very famous ancient Christian autobiography, namely, the *Confessions* of St. Augustine. Next, we will shift our focus to pagan writings and compare Aristides' dream book with another pagan autobiographical writing, namely, *Meditations* composed by the Emperor Marcus Aurelius. A comparative approach will elucidate some of the common and unique features of each of these texts as well as help us to discover some interesting aspects of these religious documents. Our goal is to address any similarities and differences between these documents both in terms of style and content. Finally, we will highlight some commonalities and differences between the *Sacred Tales* and Apuleius' *Metamorphoses*, Book XI.

Since we have already established the fact that Aristides is a religious individual, we need to clarify the type of piety that is expressed in the *Sacred Tales*. In order to do this we will need to classify the particular type of religiosity described in the *Sacred Tales*. A suitable classification system is found in the writings of William James. In *The Varieties of Religious Experience* James makes a noteworthy distinction between two basic types or classes of religious individuals.[1] On the one hand, there is the religion of the "healthy-minded" and, on the other hand, there is the religion of the "sick soul." The religion of the healthy-minded is characterized by positive values such as faith and devotion whereas the religion of the sick soul is focused upon overcoming the forces of darkness and spiritual transformation. Although there may be other types of personal religion besides these two types, and perhaps not everyone can be classified into one of these two types, nevertheless the distinction made by James has significance for our discussion of the religiosity of Aristides. Ironically, past scholarship has portrayed Aristides as an "anxious pagan" or an example of the "sick soul." Justification for such a personal characterization is based upon the multitude of physical ailments catalogued *ad infinitum* in the *Sacred Tales*. However, Aristides' clinging devotion to Asclepius clearly represents an example of the religion of "healthy-mindedness."

Contemporary examples of "healthy-minded" religion can be found in the various faith-healing and mind-cure movements. The cult of Asclepius may represent an ancient precursor to such religious phenomena. According to James, the goal of healthy-mindedness is the attainment of a feeling of "happiness" which is achieved by staying focused on the positive. Likewise, Aristides' optimistic devotion to the healing powers of Asclepius spiritually empowers him at least temporarily to overcome much of the physical pain and suffering associated with his many ailments. There have been few, if any, scholars who have recognized the positive dimension of Aristides' piety. This is most likely due to having been overwhelmed by the multitude of physical maladies and ordeals that are detailed in the text. Contrary to Judith Perkins' comments about Aristides and the *Sacred Tales* in her book, *The Suffering Self*, it is important to remember that the central topic of the *Sacred Tales* is not Aristides' physical illnesses nor his incessant suffering,

---

[1] James, W. *The Varieties of Religious Experience*, (New York, 1958). See especially ch. 3 and 4 where James discusses the religion of the healthy-minded and the sick soul.

but rather the miraculous cures experienced by him provided by his the god Asclepius.² Neither death, suffering nor the physical body are the central topics of the *Sacred Tales*. To include Aristides in a general discussion of the symbolic meaning of suffering in Late Antiquity may be appropriate. However, it implies that he belongs to the realm of the "sick soul" and de-emphasizes the optimistic and curative aspects of Aristides' religiosity and personality. Actually, most of Aristides' physical ailments were manageable through a combination of human and temple medicine and the miraculous healing power of his god. Obviously, some of this involved positive thinking on Aristides' part. In James' framework, Aristides is an example of the "once-born" who seeks religious happiness and security by staying optimistically focused upon the miraculous healing powers of Asclepius.

When we compare the religious piety on display in the *Sacred Tales* with the religiosity expressed in the Augustine's *Confessions*, we see that both texts are confessions of personal religious faith. However, there are some noteworthy differences between these two religious individuals. In contrast to Aristides, St. Augustine is probably one of the best examples of a "sick soul" in the ancient world. In a relatively short period of two centuries after the time of Aristides, the spiritual landscape had grown far much more dark and complex. A dramatic shift in perspetives had occurred, moving away from the old classical way of looking at things to a new way of perceiving the world. Augustine exemplifies the Christian perspective; life is about personal sacrifice, about "giving up" one's old self and becoming "twice-born." The plot of the *Confessions* is really the story of Augustine's spiritual transformation away from his old self to his new self. It is not an easy process. Along the way, there are many tales of sin and temptation. One such memorable story Augustine tells us is "the incident of the pears." As a boy Augustine and his companions stole some pears from a neighbor's fruit tree. Throughout his life, he continued to consider this an act of extreme wickedness. He states,

---

[2] Perkins, J. *The Suffering Self: Pain and Narrative Representation in the Early Christian Era*, (London and New York, 1995), pp. 173–177.

[I]t was foul and I loved it; I loved to perish, I loved mine own fault, not that for the sake of which I committed the fault, but my fault itself I loved. Foul soul, falling from the firmament to expulsion from Thy Presence; not seeking aught through the shame, but the shame itself.[3]

Upon reflecting on this passage from the *Confessions*, Bertrand Russell states that "He goes on like this for seven chapters, and all about the pears plucked from a tree in a boyish prank. To the modern mind, this seems morbid."[4]

The genre of religious autobiography develops in the ancient West in both the context of pagan and Christian religious traditions in roughly the same time-period and yet in each religious context something different emerges. On the surface, the *Sacred Tales* and the *Confessions* have obvious similarities and yet we are struck by differences both in terms of narrative style as well as theological outlook. Although both writers concentrate upon their relationship to the divine, this religious relationship differs for each, since each believes in a different god and each of these deities has different requirements for sustaining that relationship. For Augustine, the focus is upon the Judeo-Christian god who is a moral god, whereas for Aristides, it is Asclepius, the healer god who receives all of the attention. In the *Sacred Tales*, Aristides' religious dreams form the main content of the text yet his narration is often chaotic and confusing in its presentation. Aristides does not provide us with any overriding moral insights or "lessons learned" about his life. Unlike Augustine's self-portrayal, there is an absence of any sense of guilt whenever Aristides recollects the events of his life. Instead, Aristides is happy in simply discussing all of Asclepius' divine interventions in his life. To a modern reader who is imbued with the Judeo-Christian world-view, such an optimistic, positive outlook might seem unusually superficial and lacking in depth.

Seen in the context of ancient Mediterranean religions, the *Sacred Tales* is in many ways a standard reflection of the dominant re-

---

[3] This quotation from the *Confessions* is excerpted from B. Russell's *The History of Western Philosophy*, (New York, 1946), p. 330.

[4] Ibid.

ligious themes of his era which include a high degree of credulity, a belief in the power of the gods in human existence and a heightened interest in individual salvation. When discussing his entry into the cult of Asclepius, Aristides is really interested in talking about the origin of his illnesses as opposed to any type of spiritual transformation. Nowhere in the discussion does he portray himself as a "divided soul" or under the sway of sin prior to his association with the cult of Asclepius. Aristides' perspective on the initial events leading to his entry into the cult are seen to represent only insignificant fragmentary events in the long history of his illnesses and have little importance except in terms of forming the background related to the beginnings of his physical maladies.

Aristides' self-portrayal stands in stark opposition to St. Augustine's portrayal of himself. Augustine's heightened moral conscience serves as the guiding principle of the *Confessions*. Moral and ethical categories play little of no role in the *Sacred Tales*. However, what Aristides lacks in conceiving the universe and his place in it in ethical terms is fully compensated by his deep religious feelings for his god Asclepius. It is the articulation of his religious feelings that we are interested in exploring, not his moral perspective. Moralistic concepts are fundamental to the Christian religious perspective yet we must remember Aristides was a pagan. As Timothy Luke Johnson states,

> Aristides reveals absolutely no pessimism concerning the empirical world nor any desire to escape from the world through the shedding of the body—despite his chronically ill condition... I can count only the merest handful of places where he even touches on moral behavior... We find in him virtually no trace of religion as moral transformation.[5]

For Johnson, Aristides' piety is characterized by what he calls "participation in divine benefits." Aristides' participation in "divine benefits" consisted in his adherence to the cult of Asclepius.

As a pagan devotee of the god Asclepius, Aristides was still locked in the old classical way of seeing things; as a "healthy-

---

[5] Johnson, L. Ibid p. 63.

minded" follower of Asclepius, he lacked the spiritual angst associated with the Christian moral perspective. As Robert Smith points out,

> [T]he *Sacred Tales* give little if any hint that Aristides perceived the world to be a place where the gods were no longer active. The breakdown of the traditional pagan vision was left for others to understand and interpret.[6]

Certainly, if we perceive the essence of religion as an extension of morality, then Aristides' piety as well as his self-understanding as it appears in the *Sacred Tales* surely appears shallow and superficial in juxtaposition to Augustine's morbid self-consciousness and introspective outlook on his life. In comparison to Augustine, Aristides appears obsessive and caught up in a cycle of meaningless ritual behavior. The *Confessions* is a reflection of many of the deeply moral and spiritual doctrines of the Christian religion whereas Aristides' religiosity reminds us of a more primitive type of religious experience rooted in joyous feelings and ecstatic emotion rather than conscience and morality.

Karl Weintraub writes that Augustine was,

> [M]oved by a deeply-felt need to understand the meaning of his being and his life. The sheer act of writing is thus an act of self-orientation… By thus interlacing all the segments of time, the book reaches into that realm in which genuine autobiography lives.[7]

Augustine's life is ordered in terms of what has come to give his life meaning. Weintraub states,

> Augustine's entire assessment of life is dominated by the consciousness of his conversion experience in 386; thus, the *Confessions* belong to that type of autobiography in which one datable moment in life enables a human being

---

[6] Smith, R. p. 48. Ibid.
[7] Karl Weintraub, *The Value of the Individual*, (Chicago, Ill., 1978), p. 24.

to order all his experience retrospectively by the insight of one momentous turn.[8]

One important aspect of the genre of autobiography, especially as it appears in modern times, is that the author is writing about his own life and doing so in a way that will enable him to understand his life both in terms of its entire character and the contributions made by certain segments of his life to the entire meaning of his life-experience. Whereas this over-arching purposeful narrative structure is present in the *Confessions*, it is missing from the *Sacred Tales*. In Augustine's *Confessions* the various episodes in his youth including his relationship with his mother Monica and his father Patricus and his conversion experience all are conceived from the perspective of Christian faith so that "a feeling of movement in time, of history, a consciousness of an inward stream of focus is portrayed to his audience."[9]

It is commonly believed by many scholars that in the *Confessions*, for the first time, and largely because of the spiritual and literary merits of its author, the autobiographer tells the story of his own religious evolution. Hence, the *Confessions* are considered by most scholars to be the first genuine autobiography in the modern sense of the word. Likewise, Augustine is credited with being "the first modern man" as well as the world's first existentialist.

To be fair to Aristides, we should note that to a certain extent, the incoherence and confusing organization of his dream book reflects the special circumstances surrounding its creation. Looking into the details surrounding the creation of Aristides' diary, we find that in the prologue of S.T.I and II Aristides tells us that at first he hesitated to compose his religious narrative because of the difficulty in recalling all of the details regarding the miracles and visions witnessed by him in the cult. In S.T.I he states that for years his friends asked him to record the miraculous deeds of Asclepius, yet none of them ever convinced him of doing the impossible (το αδυνατον). He states that he had simply experienced the provi-

---

[8] Ibid., p. 25.
[9] Roy Pascal, *Design and Truth in Autobiography*, (Cambridge, Mass., 1960), p. 22.

dence of the god so often that the task of producing an accurate discussion of the material was beyond his mental and physical capabilities.[10]

Furthermore, in the prologue to Book II, Aristides tells us that in the past, his policy was to avoid discussing such divine deeds and he gives a variety of excuses for failing to compose anything. However, he tells us that after many years, dream visions compel him to speak. Many of his dreams were completely forgotten; in some cases his dreams were either not written down at the time they were dreamt, and in certain cases his notes about his dreams were lost through the years. His remaining notes about his dreams contained about three hundred thousand lines and this material was completely unorganized and not easy to put in chronological sequence. As a result, much of the *Sacred Tales* is presented in a summary fashion and organized topographically as opposed to chronologically.[11]

Based upon this data we can understand why the *Sacred Tales* was written in a rather carefree manner without much thought to chronological structure. It might be claimed that Aristides lacked the historical consciousness to be overly concerned with the development of his own religious identity. Misch posits that "the full reality of the unique life of the soul was not revealed to the ancients."[12] Aristides was no exception. Misch's assessment of the *Sacred Tales* is decidedly negative; Aristides account is "confused, even absurd, to those in search of anything of human significance—a category which cannot be applied here."[13] Misch's harsh appraisal of Aristides' autobiographical work is grounded upon the conclusion that Aristides did not show enough interest in the temporal flow of his experience nor did he make any connections between his individual experiences and events of his life and the overall direction of his life. Instead, Aristides is satisfied using analogy to move from one topic to another, shifting back and forth from one time period to another. In the final analysis, Aristides

---

[10] S.T.I.1–4.
[11] S.T.II.3.
[12] Misch, op. cit., vol. 1, p. 66.
[13] Misch, op. cit., p. 504.

fails to trace the teleology of his life-experience. Of course, all of this is quite different from Augustine's *Confessions*, which consists of a "history of the soul."

Should we agree with Misch's assessment of the *Sacred Tales*? Misch's appraisal of the text reflects the Judeo-Christian presupposition that autobiography needs to be a "history of the soul" and yet such values would be alien to a pagan of the Greco-Roman world view. As Werner Jaeger states in his review of Misch's book,

> [W]hat appears in our modern perspective as a strange self-limitation of ancient autobiography... begins to look quite logical and natural within the context of its own society and intellectual tradition.[14]

PAGAN AND CHRISTIAN SICK SOULS: MARCUS AURELIUS AND ST. PAUL

The subject-matter of religious experience on the individual plane of human existence is presented in a number of pagan documents dating from Hellenistic and Roman times,[15] although not all forms of pagan religiosity in Greco-Roman times are comparable to the once-born form of piety displayed in the *Sacred Tales*. Perhaps one of the loftiest pieces of personal reflection recorded in pagan literature appears in the second century CE, namely the *Meditations* of Marcus Aurelius. Marcus is an excellent example of a sick soul but instead of appearing in the context of Christianity, we now find it in the context of the philosophical movement known as Stoicism.

The quality of detachment and pessimism that characterizes much of Marcus' attitude about life makes him a much better ex-

---

[14] Werner Jaeger, "A Review of a History of Autobiography in Antiquity," *Speculum*, vol. 23, (1953), p. 408.

[15] See for example Apuleius, *The Golden Ass*, 4th ed., translated by Jack Lindsey, (Bloomington and London, 1974) especially ch. XI; an excellent translation and commentary of Book XI is provided by H. Gwyn Griffiths, *The Isis Book*, (Leiden, 1975); another example of personal religion in the Hellenistic-Roman period can be found in the writings of Philo of Alexandria who depicts himself in a state of ecstasy while engaged in his exegetical studies. Cf. Philo, *De Migrations Abrahami*, 34–35; Misch, op. cit., vol. II, p. 497.

ample of an "anxious pagan" than Aristides. In the *Meditations* Marcus makes a number of personal allusions to his own loneliness as the emperor of Rome. As a Stoic, Marcus has a sense of restraint and withdrawal from the world of the senses and finds strength in the knowledge that there exists a principle of divine order permeating the fabric of the universe. In comparison to Aristides' singular focus on his religious dream visions, Marcus' piety can be characterized as an expression of his interest in theological doctrines such as those found in the philosophical school of Stoicism. At one point he writes, "for nowhere can a man find a retreat more full of peace or more full from care than his own soul" (*Med* 4.3). Like Aristides, Marcus does not present a historical overview of his life. Instead, Marcus gives us a rather limited picture of his personal history which contains a few memories of his teachers, family relatives and friends. Because Marcus accepted Plato's view that this world is filled with evil and is in a state of "becoming" and lacks permanence, he tended to emphasize certain negative feelings toward the world of the flesh and especially the body. In contrast with this negative attitude towards the physical world, Marcus focused many of his writings upon other-worldly pursuits. Thus, he writes,

> [O]f the life of man the duration is but a point, its substance streaming away, its perception dim, the fabric of the entire body prone to decay, and the soul is a vortex and fortune incalculable, and fame uncertain. (*Med* 2.17)

Like the *Sacred Tales*, the *Meditations* do not attempt to map out a life-history of the emperor. However, it would be incorrect to assume that the *Meditations* do not contain a personal dimension. Although some scholars doubt whether the *Meditations* reveal Marcus' innermost thoughts, no one has been able to successfully argue that the text is merely a moral treatise.[16] The hidden autobiographical dimension of the text can be seen in certain aspects. Like the *Sacred Tales*, the *Meditations* are loosely organized. Moreover, the topic of

---

[16] P. A. Brunt, "Marcus Aurelius and His Meditations," *Journal of Roman Studies*, vol. 64, (1974), pp. 1–20; see also Samuel Dill, *Roman Society From Nero to Marcus Aurelius*, (London, 1911), p. 390.

discussion often changes quickly and inexplicably, giving the impression that Marcus is ruminating upon various philosophical topics for his own personal reasons rather than presenting to the public a systematic exposition of the material.

A similar kind of dark pessimism is found in the writings of the Gnostics. Many Gnostic texts take a negative position regarding earthly human life and our place in this world. For example, in the autobiographical prologue of the text *Zostrianos* we read that,

> after I mentally abandoned my inner corporeal darkness, psychical chaos, and dark, lustful, femininity with which I was unconcerned, and after I had discovered the boundlessness of my materialism and reproved the dead creation within me as well as the perceptible divine world ruler, I powerfully proclaimed wholeness to those with unrelated parts.

A similar type of pessimism is also identifiable, although on a much more limited basis, in the letters of St Paul.[17]

If we peruse Paul's letters, we repeatedly find a concern with the powers of sin. Although he frequently talks in general terms about the weakness of the flesh, Paul was not particularly revealing about the role of sin in his own life. In this connection, we should mention that although Romans 7 has been interpreted by many to be a passage where Paul is speaking autobiographically about the law and sin, in fact the passage is really a statement about the objective condition of man in general under the Torah. In his book *Romans 7 and the Conversion of Paul*, Werner Kummel refutes the contention that Romans 7:7–25 is an autobiographical statement.[18] Likewise, in his article "Paul and the Introspective Conscience of the West," Krister Stendahl maintains that Romans 7 is a discussion of the law and even though Paul uses the personal pronoun "I" in no way is Paul talking about his own personal ego under the

---

[17] *Zostrianos*, trans. John Turner in *The Nag Hammadi Scriptures*, edited by Marvin Meyer (New York, 2007), p. 545.

[18] Werner Kummel, *Romer 7 und Das Bild des Menschen in Neuen Testament*, (Munchen, 1974).

old law of the Torah.[19] In Philippians 3 Paul discusses his conversion and he does not mention any difficulty in fulfilling the law. Likewise, in the aftermath of Paul's conversion, there is no mention of his consciousness of being a sinner. In 1 Corinthians 9.27, Paul is aware of a struggle with his body yet he does not display the signs of a troubled conscience.

In comparison to Aristides' healthy-mindedness, Christian writers such as Paul and Augustine portray the human condition to be permeated by self-doubt, sinful tendencies and temptation. According to these writers, the main problem of human existence concerns the unrelenting struggle between the forces of good and evil. Likewise, the Stoic emperor Marcus Aurelius presents a far more detached and pessimistic attitude towards life in this world than what is presented in the *Sacred Tales*. As a typical Greco-Roman pagan, Aristides was not really conscious of the "problem of evil" and therefore such a conception of evil did not have any relevance for his self-understanding or his orientation towards his life-situation. As a result, Aristides had no interest in the practice of asceticism.

Unlike many of his era, Aristides lacked the religious sense of asceticism and withdrawal from the world even though he practiced a kind of fasting and bathing for therapeutic reasons. In Peter Brown's words, he did not have,

> [W]hat contemporaries of other classes and regions were groping toward in their radical religious beliefs: a religious means of expressing, by drastic gestures of protest or renunciation, such as the publicizing of visions to their fellow believers or the adoption of harsh regimes of fasting… that sense of separateness which went with a sense of superiority based upon a closeness to the di-

---

[19] Krister Stendahl, "Paul and the Introspective Conscience of the West," in *The Writings of St. Paul*, ed. Wayne Meeks, (New York, 1972), p. 433.

vine... he (Aristides) refused to draw on the power of the symbol in making sense of his regime.[20]

When discussing his bathing practices and many fasts, Aristides failed to draw upon religious symbolism, that is, "public, historically created vehicles of reasoning, perception, feeling and understanding."[21] In Peter Brown's words "for Aristides, the nagging question of 'to bathe or not to bathe' remained private, and his rejection of baths remained locked away in the labyrinthine courses of his illness."[22]

Aristides' religiosity reminds us of a more primitive type of religious experience rooted in feeling and emotion rather than morality. Thus, it seems appropriate to compare Aristides' *Sacred Tales* on its own terms to another type of autobiography exhibiting a similar type of religious enthusiasm and zeal as opposed to the more introspective kind of religious behavior found in such documents as the *Meditations* and the *Confessions*. Such a document is found in another pagan composition, namely, Book XI of the *Metamorphoses*.

THE SACRED TALES IN COMPARISON TO THE METAMORPHOSES

The *Metamorphoses* tells the satirical story of Lucius who is magically transformed into a donkey and journeys around the Roman Empire having one adventure after the other. Book XI tells the tale of Lucius' initiation into the cult of Isis. Lucius describes an appearance of Isis by referring to her radiant image and her robe embroidered with gleaming stars and a fiery half-moon. Lucius' portrayal of Isis emphasizes her marvelous beauty. Lucius states "I saw the sun flashing with bright effulgence."[23] A similar comment is made by Porphyry who states that the human eye cannot bear the bright

---

[20] Peter Brown, *The Making of Late Antiquity*, (Cambridge, Mass, 1978) pp. 43–44.
[21] Brown, op. cit., p. 45.
[22] Ibid.
[23] Apuleius, *Metamorphoses* XI 23, trans. H. Gwyn Griffiths, *The Isis Book*, (Leiden, 1975), p. 99.

light of divine epiphanies.²⁴ Likewise, the philosopher Proclus notes that during initiation rites into the mysteries there poured forth a light from the gods which sometimes took human shape, and other times was formless.²⁵

Similar to the above mentioned passages, Aristides states in S.T. III 46 that Isis appeared to him and the presence of light is mentioned. In the same passage we are informed that Sarapis also appeared on the same night as well as Asclepius. Both were marvelous in their beauty and magnitude and like one another in some ways. We should also note that several other parallels exist between the *Sacred Tales* and Book XI of Lucius' *Metamorphoses*.

Boulanger makes a brief observation in his study on Aristides that "il y a d'ailleurs *Discours Sacres* et le dernier livre *de Metamorphoses*."²⁶ Unfortunately, Boulanger does not specify in detail what these two texts have in common. In comparing the two texts we should remember that Book XI of the *Metamorphoses* deals with Lucius' initiation into the mysteries of Isis. Even though Aristides' religiosity shares some things in common with Lucius' religiosity, it does not mean that Aristides belonged to a mystery-religion nor does it mean that there existed any direct historical connection between the two figures. Nevertheless, it is fair to say that Aristides' religious experience and its symbolic articulation has many phenomenological similarities with the experience of one initiate of the mysteries of Isis, namely, Lucius. However, there are distinct theological differences between the cult of Asclepius and the mystery-religions in general and the cult of Asclepius was not a mystery religion. Although many Eastern religious cults took the appearance of mysteries, the worship of Asclepius in the Greco-Roman world did not include any initiatory rituals that could be termed "myster-

---

[24] Porphyry, De Mysteriis II.8; S. Angus, *The Mystery Religions and Christianity*, (New York, 1925), p. 136.

[25] Proclus, In Plat. Remp. I cf. Angus, op. cit., p. 136. See also *The Theological Dictionary of the N.T.*, ed. Kittel, vol. 9, p. 278 and 310f.

[26] Boulanger, Andre, *Aelius Aristides et la Sophistique dans la province d'Asia*, (Paris, 1923), p. 202f.

ies" in which soteriological knowledge was revealed to the initiate.[27] Despite the vague metaphorical references to the τελετή in the *Sacred Tales*, Asclepius did not offer his devotees the blessings of immortality, unlike the initiates of the Eleusinian mysteries. Nevertheless, Aristides' religious experience and its symbolic articulation has some similarities with the religious experiences of Lucius.

In general, the tone of Lucius' adoration of Isis bears some resemblance to the devotion of Aristides to Asclepius. Just as Aristides lived in the temple precincts for two years following his initial entry into the cult of Asclepius, likewise Lucius also lived in the temple of Isis as a *cultor inseparabilis*.[28] During this period, Lucius had many visions just as Aristides did. Both Lucius and Aristides are involved in a similar type of religious experience consisting of elements of religious revelation and devotion. Each individual claims to have received revelations from the deity; in the case of Aristides we are dealing with a member of a healing cult as opposed to an initiate of a mystery-cult.

Although the *Metamorphoses* is a romantic novel, most scholars believe that the details of the initiation ritual presented in Book XI are based upon the actual personal experiences of Apuleius in the cult of Isis.[29] Both Aristides and Apuleius refer to the idea that miraculous phenomena cannot be adequately described in words. The appearance of this motif in each text does not necessarily imply an historical influence since ineffability is a universal religious phenomenon. Upon seeing Isis in his dream, Lucius states,

> I will try to communicate to you her wonderful appearance if the poverty of human speech affords me the means of description or if the deity herself lends me her rich store of rhetorical eloquence.[30]

---

[27] Franz Cumont, *The Oriental Religions in Roman Paganism*, 2nd ed., (New York, 1956), p. 205.
[28] Griffiths, *The Isis Book*, op. cit., p. 319; *Meta.*19.
[29] Griffiths, *The Isis Book* op. cit., pp. 1–7.
[30] Apuleius, *Meta*, Book II.3, trans., Griffiths, op. cit., p. 73.

Likewise, Aristides admits that he could never do justice to the miracles of Asclepius, even if his literary powers exceeded the limits of "all human strength, speech and wisdom."[31]

Another parallel concerns "special election." Apuleius states,

> [B]ut especially remember, and ever hold enshrined deep in your heart, that the remaining course of your life, even to the limit of your last breath, is dedicated to me. Nor is it wrong that you should devote to her, by whose favor you shall return to men, the rest of your life. You shall live indeed a happy man, you shall live full of glory in my protection.[32]

Similarly, Aristides tells us that Asclepius prolonged his life,[33] and that a foster child died in exchange for the life of Aristides.[34] Furthermore, Aristides refers to his "special election" in a variety of terms. In one instance, Aristides dreams that he is standing with a group in the temple. When the group begins to leave, the god indicates for Aristides to remain in the temple. Being delighted with the honor, Aristides shouts out, εις (meaning "The One"). Asclepius replies, σύ εἶ (meaning "It is You").[35] We are told that Asclepius desired to change the condition of Aristides' mind so that he would be able to associate with the god and thus be superior to the lot of men.[36] Aristides is given a new name—Theodorus—yet unlike Lucius he does not receive the blessings of immortality, only the promise of physical well-being.

Just as Lucius describes Isis as possessing a marvelous beauty, Aristides states in S.T.I.46 that he saw Athena in a dream standing before him with her aegis and was marvelous in her beauty and magnitude. Again, the deity is portrayed as objectively standing before the bed of Aristides, just as Asclepius does in S.T.II.18. However, in his dream of Athena, Aristides actually wakens from

---

[31] S.T.I.1.
[32] Griffiths, op. cit., p. 77; *Meta*, 6.
[33] S.T.III.46.
[34] Ibid.
[35] S.T.IV.51
[36] S.T.IV.52.

his sleep and continues to see her and points her out to his two friends and foster sister standing by his bed. His companions thought he was delirious until they observed that his strength was returning and they learned of her medical prescriptions.[37]

In many of the epiphanies of Asclepius described in the *Sacred Tales*, the deity appears as very handsome, bearded, and with the imposing figure of Zeus. This description of Asclepius corresponds nicely with some of his sculptural depictions. The vocabulary Aristides uses to describe his dreams reflects a certain intimacy he had with his nocturnal visions. Many of his god-sent dreams are characterized by their clarity (εναργής) or the direct presence of the deity. Frequently the term δοκειν is used to introduce a dream vision, which stresses the vividness of the dream. He often employs the word ὄψις or "vision" to describe a vision. In S.T.II.41 the phrase ἔδοξα ὡς ὄναρ is used to describe the state between sleep and waking characterized by unusually clear dreams. The word ὕπαρ or "waking vision" is used in some passages.

The phrase "consciousness of a presence" could be used to describe Aristides' spiritual experience as it appears in S.T.II.32. He tells us that "there was a seeming as it were, to touch him and to perceive that he himself had come."[38] Aristides tells us he heard some things (ὡς ὄναρ) and other things (ὡς ὕπαρ).[39] His hair stood on end and he cried tears of joy. While delirious and in bed he states that he was conscious of himself as if he were someone else. Subsequently he witnessed an appearance of Athena and Asclepius.

Many of Aristides' most intense religious experiences occurred to him while in a semi-conscious state. This type of religious experience is discussed in William James' classic study *The Varieties of Religious Experience*. Several examples are cited of individuals who are only half awake and who have experienced a kind of spiritual presence. On this basis, James concludes that in man's psyche there exists

---

[37] S.T.II.32.see also S.T.I.22, I30, IV.56 and V.64.
[38] S.T.II.32.
[39] S.T.II.33.

> [A] sense of reality, a feeling of objective presence, a perception of what we may call something there, more deep and more general than any of the special and particular senses by which the current psychology supposes existent realities to be originally revealed.[40]

The author of the Imouthes text speaks of receiving a revelation while his mind is hovering between the state of sleep and wakefulness. Iamblichus refers to some dreams as *theopemotoi* or "sent from god". These dreams occur at the time when an individual is about to wake up. Macrobius speaks of the apparition descending upon the person in the moment between wakefulness and slumber in the so-called "first cloud of sleep." A similar type of visionary experience was reported by W. B. Yeats in the *Celtic Twilight*. Yeats describes one of his own waking visions as, "a young man and girl dressed in olive-green raiment cut like old Greek raiment... standing at my bedside."[41] Several other examples of such a phenomenon can be located in the history of mysticism.

Comparison of the *Sacred Tales* with Book XI of the *Metamorphoses* reinforces our point of view about the depth and sincerity of Aristides' piety. Both Aristides and Lucius had genuinely intense religious feelings, and both texts manifest a number of phenomenological parallels underscoring the genuineness of the religious experiences described in each text. Unlike our previous comparison of *Sacred Tales* with the *Confessions* and the *Meditations*, when we compare the *Metamorphoses* with Aristides' dream diary, the similarities between the texts increases our appreciation of each text in respect to the depth and genuineness of the religiosity portrayed. The primary reason for this is due to the fact that we are comparing two texts belonging to the same religious and social environments, namely the Greco-Roman religious cults. Thus, rather than judging one religious text according to the religious and social values of the other text, we are dealing with two texts, each of which

---

[40] William James, *The Varieties of Religious Experience*, Mentor paperback ed., (New York, 1958), p. 62.

[41] W. B. Yeats, "The Celtic Twilight," in *Mythologies*, (New York, 1969), p. 68.

share similar spiritual perspectives. As a result, neither text is relegated to an inferior position but instead complements the other. Our comparative analysis clarifies an important point, namely, that Aristides is not quite as abnormal or anxious as some have thought. When viewed in the right context, Aristides does not appear as a "sick soul" but rather as a healthy-minded religious person, an example of *homo religiosus*.

CHAPTER FOUR: DREAMS AND MIRACLES IN THE SACRED TALES

THE SACRED TALES AND RELIGIOUS ARETALOGY

Human awareness of the sacred and its symbolic articulation do not occur in a cultural vacuum but rather are conditioned and influenced by the culture and society in which they occur. The *Sacred Tales* reflects a number of features of ancient miracle literature. Not only can the text be studied in the context of ancient autobiography, but it can also be studied as an example of religious aretalogy. Aretalogy may be defined as a type of ancient literature in which the miraculous deeds of the god are proclaimed. This type of writing was fairly common in antiquity.

The language and narrative content found in the *Sacred Tales* reveal parallels and similarities in terms of linguistics and narrative content to both the Epidaurian inscriptional evidence as well as several of the miracle stories found in the N.T. gospels. As we indicated in Chapter Three during our discussion of Book XI of the *Metamorphoses*, in spite of the numerous phenomenological parallels existing between our text and the other texts under consideration, this does not necessarily imply any direct historical dependency between the texts. However, these textual parallels underscore the fact that Aristides' piety is neither a one-of-a-kind phenomenon nor should his spiritual diary be understood outside of the confines of ancient Western religions in general.

The French scholar Andre Boulanger was the first student of the *Sacred Tales* to classify it as an example of the many, popular aretalogical works dealing with the subject matter of Providence, miracles, and apparitions. Similar subjects are treated by a number of ancient authors including Aelian and others.[1] The *Sacred Tales* can be fruitfully studied as an example of religious aretalogy since it has unmistakable similarities both in language and content to the miracle literature found in Greco-Roman and early Christian literature. In this sense, Aristides shares the religious aretalogist's desire to establish the reality of the god's wondrous powers by enumerating the miraculous interventions of the god. In doing so, the religious aretalogist bears witness to their faith in the god.

Accounts of the life of a "divine man" or *theos aner* are associated with aretalogy. However, although the *Sacred Tales* can be properly understood as an example of religious aretalogy, we must remember that it does not present an account of a *theos aner* or "divine man." Such accounts are found in the writings of Plato in his biographical narrative of Socrates as well as in Philo's biography of Moses.

Furthermore, just as "autobiography" was not distinguished as a literary genre in ancient times, many modern scholars, such as Martin Nilsson, and more recently David Tiede and Howard Kee, have argued that there is no evidence to support the claim that aretalogy was a distinct genre of ancient literature and possessed a definitive number of finite features.[2] Kee criticizes Moses Hadas' definition of aretalogy as "a formal account of a remarkable career of an impressive teacher that was used as the basis for moral instruction."[3] Kee states that Philostratus' description of Apollonius of Tyana in his *Life of Apollonius of Tyana* fails to establish a pattern "of sufficient precision to be called a literary genre."[4] Even though Hadas' definition of aretalogy is descriptive of Luke's portrayal of the figure of Jesus, there are difficulties with this definition in connection to the *Sacred Tales*. To be sure, Hadas' definition of aretalogy

---

[1] Andre Boulanger, *Aelius Aristides et la Sophistique dans la province d'Asia*, op. cit., p. 163.

[2] See Martin Nilsson, *Geschichte der Griechischen Religion*, op. cit., vol. II, p. 228; David Tiede, *The Charismatic Figure as Miracle Worker*, op. cit., p. 1.

[3] Howard Kee, "Aretalogy and Gospel," *Journal of Biblical Literature*, vol. 92, (Sept., 1973), pp. 402–422

[4] Kee, op. cit., p. 407. See also Moses Hadas and Morton Smith, *Heroes and Gods: Spiritual Biographies in Antiquity* (New York, 1965), p. 3.

has no applicability to Aristides' *Sacred Tales* since he does not reveal the events of his life for the purpose of "moral instruction." As we have previously stated, Aristides' self-presentation is devoid of a moral perspective and he does not share the morbid self-consciousness that typifies the Augustinian perspective.

Nevertheless, the text can be considered an example of aretalogy if we broaden our definition of the term. A broader definition of the term "aretalogy" as being a collection of miracles stories has been suggested by Nilsson and Morton Smith.[5] Such a definition is far more inclusive of the diverse literary texts existing in ancient Mediterranean religious environments and could certainly be used to categorize the *Sacred Tales* as an example of aretalogy. Smith notes that there is no extant text where the term "aretalogy" is used in the title. However, there is a text entitled Διος Ηλιου μεγαλου ξαραπιδος αρετη or *A Miracle of Zeus Helios great Sarapis*.[6] Accordingly, Smith states that an aretalogy involved the telling of miracle stories and their chief function was to propagandize the glorious deeds of the god.[7] It is important to remember that the *Sacred Tales* is a by-product of Aristides' close association with the cult of Asclepius. Although he was not an official member of the priestly community at Pergamum, he did use his rhetorical skills to proclaim the wondrous deeds of the god.

In this regard, we must remember that the recitation of miracles was an official duty of temple priests in ancient Mediterranean religious cults including the cult of Asclepius. In one Delian inscription, priestly duties appear to include dream interpretation. In this inscription, the word αρεταλογος and ονειροκριτης are mentioned together, thus linking the idea of proclaiming the virtues of the god and interpreting dreams.[8] The inscription is making reference to a cult official whose primary function was two-fold: to pro-

---

[5] Nilsson, op. cit., pp. 228–229; Morton Smith, "Prolegomena to Aretalogies, Divine Men and Gospel," *Journal of Biblical Literature*, vol. 90, (1971), p. 176.

[6] Smith, op. cit., p. 176; Oxy. Pap.11, 1382, lines 22ff. 1.

[7] Ibid.

[8] Tiede, op. cit., p. 104; I.G.11.4.2072; S. Reinach, "Les Aretalogues dans l'antiquite," *Bulletin de_correspondence hellenique*, vol. 9, (1885); p. 157f.

claim the glorious deeds of the deity and to decipher the hidden messages of god-sent dreams. Since one priestly individual can be responsible for both interpreting dreams and proclaiming the god's miraculous actions in the world, the scholar David Tiede concludes that the aretalogist, "proclaims miracles and furthermore dreams are regarded by the aretalogist as miracles."[9]

In the ancient West, miracles are often told in a cultic context and many of the technical terms associated with this type of literature find their way into the *Sacred Tales*. However, this is not true in respect to all the terminology that was used. In certain cases, some terms appear in one source but are absent in other sources. For example, one common term used in aretalogical literature, αρετη, is not present in the Epidaurian inscriptions.[10] Tiede mentions that Isyllus of the fourth century BCE used the term in describing Asclepius' divine power.[11] Tiede states that the citations from Isyllus and the Epidaurian inscriptions indicate that those who proclaimed the miracles of Asclepius were also bearing witness to the αρεταί of the god. In this sense, it is valid to refer to the Epidaurian temple record as a rather lengthy "aretalogy of Asclepius."[12] Just as the term αρετη is absent from the multitude of inscriptional evidence from Epidaurus, likewise the term is never used by Aristides in the *Sacred Tales*. Instead, Aristides uses the term αγωνίσματα, which can be translated as "achievements." Thus, in S.T.1.1 he refers to the "achievements of the savior" which is clearly comparable to the usage of the term αρετη or "miracle." Whereas the commentator Behr states the term αγωνισματα is a word used in rhetorical circles, Festugiere argues that it is absurd to suggest a rhetorical usage of the term in reference to this passage.[13]

---

[9] Tiede, op. cit., p. 11.

[10] Tiede, op. cit., p. 7. For Pausanias' description of the Epidaurian stellae, see Edelstein, op. cit., p. 1 and p. 5.

[11] Tiede, op. cit. p. 9, I.G.IV, 1, N.128, v. 57–79; Edelstein, *Asclepius*, op. cit., vol. 1, p. 143 T.295.

[12] Tiede, op. cit., p. 8.

[13] A. J. Festugiere, "Sur les Discours Sacres d'Aelius Aristide," *Etudes d'Histoir et de Philologie*, op. cit., p. 118.

Aristides used many of the terms found in the miracle literature of the ancient West. For example, the word εργον in the sense of work or deed is used in S.T.II.1 to describe Asclepius' miraculous powers.[14] In S.T.IV.17 a healing formula is called a "marvelous deed of the god" (εργον του Θεου Θαυμαστον). The term has reference in Hellenistic Judaism and the New Testament to God's divine action in the world. The *Theological Dictionary of the New Testament* cites passages such as Exod 34:10 and Deut 3:24 to show that God's εργα is sometimes understood to be equivalent with the term "miracle." Perhaps more relevant for our understanding of Aristides' usage of the term εργον is the Gospel of John's usage to describe "God's saving acts through Christ."[15] In this context, the term is used to denote the miracles performed by Jesus.

Another aretalogical term used by Aristides in the *Sacred Tales* is the word Θαυμαστος, meaning "wonderful" or "marvelous." Aristides' divine dreams are said to be Θαυμαστος in S.T.II.15. In S.T.II.30 the notion of wonder is connected with the δυναμις of the god. In S.T.II.55 Asclepius' power is said to be Θαυμαστα because it reveal his δυναμις.[16] In S.T.V 55 Aristides experiences a marvelous warmth ultimately induced by the god. Likewise, in Homer's *Odyssey* 9.190 Θαυμα is used to mean "miracle." The word also appears in various contexts in the legends of Heracles and elsewhere in the Greek tradition. In ancient religious texts the appearance of a god causes man to experience terror and wonder in the presence of the sacred.[17] In the N.T. the word most frequently appears in the Gospel of Luke in the context of the miracle stories. Dibelius notes that the term is used by Luke usually towards the

---

[14] S.T.I.3; I.67; I.74; II.2.

[15] Kittel, *The Theological Dictionary of the New Testament*, op. cit., p. 642. See John 5:20,36; 7:3,21; 9:3; 4:10,25,32,37,38.

[16] See also S.T.II.74, II.82,III.40, IV.1, IV.39,40

[17] Kittel, op. cit., vol. 3, p. 28. See Hom., *Od.* 1.323, 19, 36; II3, 398, Hom. *Hymn to Ap.* 135; Vergil, Aen. III, 172; Lk. 24:41; Plato, *Phaedr.* 257c; Job 37:1; Lucian, "A True Story," 2.41, Philostratus, *Life of Apollonius*, I.38, 4.45

end of a story when the reaction of the crowd witnessing the miracle is described.[18]

The term δυναμις is used by Aristides to describe the mighty powers of Asclepius' power.[19] Just like εργον and Θαυμαστος, the word δυναμις has traditional associations with miracle literature of antiquity. The Imuthes-Aesculapius Pap. makes reference to the δυναμις of Asclepius, that is the "mighty deeds of the gods."[20] This text also uses the term αρετη ("virtue") in the following passage.

> When she had recovered herself she tried still trembling to wake me, and finding that the fever had left her and that much sweat was pouring off me, did reverence to the manifestation of the god... When I spoke with her, she wished to declare the virtue of the god, but I anticipating her told her all myself; for everything that she saw in the vision appeared to me in dreams.[21]

Similarly, the miracles of Jesus are described in the Synoptic gospels using the term δυναμις.[22]

Religious fear is a key element in the phenomenology of Aristides' religious experience. At the end of *Sacred Tales* III Aristides

---

[18] See Kittel, op. cit., vol. 3, p. 37. See Luke 11:14, 9:43 b; see also Matt 5:20. Kittel writes that in many cases in the gospels "it is obvious that the purpose of the narration and author is not to describe the historical and psychological impression made by Jesus on the crowd, but rather to use the motif of astonishment as a provisional means to direct the interest of the reader to the significance of the event." Kittel, op. cit., vol. 3, p. 37. The meaning of the event can only be grasped if we "adopt the standpoint of the Christian community considering the whole history of salvation." Ibid. For an example of the spectator's reaction of the amazement at seeing an instance of the providence of a god, see S.T.I.6; II.22, and II.34.

[19] S.T.II.30, 55.

[20] *The Oxy. Pap. XI*, 1381, line 42, trans. Grenfell and Hunt, (London, 1915), p. 226.

[21] *The Oxy. Pap. XI*, 1381, trans. Grenfell and Hunt, op. cit., p. 231.

[22] Kittel, op. cit., vol. 2, p. 299f. See Matt 11:20f, 13:58 (Matt 6:2,5), Luke 19:37, Acts 2:22. In Matt 13:54 the δυναμις of Jesus brings astonishment to the spectators.

tells us about his visions of the underworld occurring immediately after the death of his friend Zosimus. In these visions, Aristides is told by the gods Isis and Sarapis to give up his despair over his friend's death and subsequently in the vision Aristides' confrontation with the gods produces in him a "marvelous terror," (εκπηλξιν Θαυμαστην). Apparently, in this passage Aristides is describing a religious fear as opposed to normal human fear which Aristides refers to in other passages in the *Sacred Tales*. The vision is described as a τελετη. Similarly, in S.T.II.28 Aristides experiences a feeling of harmony after performing a series of religious rituals designed to avert his own death. In his vision, Asclepius tells him that he would die in two days unless he dug a trench and performed certain sacrifices as well as tossed some coins into the river. Aristides states that the performance of these actions made him feel as if he were performing a religious initiation since he was filled with fear and optimism. Once again the term τελετη is used. Elsewhere in the *Sacred Tales*, mystery terminology is employed when Aristides describes his inner feelings while performing various rituals.[23] Aristides describes a feeling of joy and optimism coupled with a fear that he would always be sick with all of his many illnesses.

Aristides' metaphorical use of mystery-terminology such as the word τελετη in connection to his descriptions of his inner psychological experiences as a participant in the cult of Asclepius should not lead us to suppose that this cult was a mystery religion. The Jungian psychotherapist C. A. Meier links the rite of incubation to the mystery religions in his book *Ancient Incubation and Modern Psychotherapy*. Meier argues that dreams play a central role in the mystery religions in that new initiates often are called to the initiation by dream. Other connections are made such as the fact that the goddess Demeter was worshipped as a goddess of healing at Pergamum[24] and that Pausanias speaks of a festival celebrating As-

---

[23] S.T.IV.7. Nock discusses Aristides' use of mystery terminology in *Early Christianity and its Hellenistic Background*, (New York, 1964), pp. 116–121.

[24] C. A. Meier, *Ancient Incubation and Modern Psychotherapy*, trans. Monica Curtis, (Evanston, 1987) p. 117.

clepius' initiation into the mysteries of Eleusis.[25] However, in spite of these and other syncretistic phenomena linking these two cults, there are some pronounced theological differences between these two religious cults including the fact that the cult of Asclepius did not include any initiatory rituals similar to "mysteries" in which soteriological knowledge was revealed to the initiate. In the cult of Asclepius, salvation was defined in terms of physical healing. Asclepius did not offer his devotees the blessings of immortality, unlike the initiates in the Eleusinian mysteries. As we have already pointed out in an earlier chapter, several parallels exist between Lucian's account of his initiation into the Eleusinian mysteries detailed in Book XI of the *Metamorphoses* and Aristides' religious dream diary; nevertheless, we must be careful not to make too much of them.

The marvelous terror experienced by Aristides in his visions is comparable to what others have made reference to when confronting the sacred. Rudolf Otto states that when confronting the sacred the human response is usually one of "religious fear before the fascinating mystery (*mysterium fascinans*)."[26] Φοβος is often the response of *homo religiosus* in the presence of an epiphany of the divine. In the N.T. Synoptic gospels, religious fear appears as a motif in the description of those bearing witness to the resurrection and the miracles of Jesus.[27] The *Theological Dictionary of the N.T.* points out that

---

[25] Pausanias II.26.8; Meier op. cit., p. 117; likewise Philostratus writes that "it was the day of Epidauria. On this day the Athenians were accustomed to carry out the initiations after the *prorrheis* (predictions) and the *hiereia* (festivals).This was instituted on account of Asclepius, because they had initiated him in his lifetime, when he came from Epidaurus, although the celebration of the mysteries had already reached an advanced stage." Philostratus, *Life of Apollonius of Tyana*, IV, 18, op. cit., Meier, p. 118.

[26] Rudolph Otto, *The Idea of the Holy*, trans. John Harvey, (London, 1958).

[27] Kittel, op. cit., v. 9, p. 194; for instances of religious fear in the Greco-Roman tradition see Homer II.20, 130f; *Od.* 1.323, Eur, *Ion* 1549f; *Oxy. Pap.* X, 1242, 53; Luc. *Demon.* 5.11, Icaromenipp., I; *Philops.* 12, etc.; epiphany-fear is discussed by O. Weinreich, *Antike Heilungswunde*, op. cit.

"epiphany-fear" is a regular element in Hellenistic aretalogy and numerous N.T. miracle stories.[28]

If we are correct in using a broad definition of the term "aretalogy" as "a collection of miracle stories," then it logically follows from this that the telling of miracle stories in ancient literature would occur in a variety of contexts. In fact, ancient literature contains an abundance of such material occurring in poetry, biography, religious writings and historiography. Next, we will compare the *Sacred Tales* with some of these other texts in order to note similarities in terms of style and content.

The Epidaurian inscriptions are a useful source of information about ancient healing cults. They also contain a number of parallels with Aristides' dream diary.[29] Written sometime during the last half of the fourth century BCE, these inscriptions were allegedly written by patients of the temple of Asclepius, although most modern scholars believe that the testimony in these inscriptions reveals the presence of priestly editing.[30] The inscriptions follow a distinct format which is somewhat reminiscent of the *Sacred Tales*. The account usually begins with a description of the individual's ailment, including the nature, seriousness, and duration of the ailment. Following this, there is a discussion of the god's intervention in the person's dream. Usually, the god heals the person in the dream itself. The account concludes with some discussion of the marvelous effects of the cure, including demonstration of the reality of the cure.

Unlike the Epidaurian inscriptions, the miraculous healings depicted in the *Sacred Tales* usually involve the performance of divine prescriptions as opposed to emanating directly from the god in a dream. This reflects a fundamental change. In classical times, the god heals his devotees directly in dreams whereas in later Hellenistic times the god heals his patients through the use of divine prescriptions which are performed in the waking state. On occa-

---

[28] Kittel, op. cit., v. 9, p. 194.

[29] For the text and translation see Edelstein, *Asclepius*, op. cit., vol. 1, p. 221f.

[30] Herzog discusses the priestly redaction in *Die Wunderheilungen von Epidauros*, Philologus Suppl. (Leipzig, 1931), p. 2, 44.

sion, Asclepius would appear to Aristides in his dreams and perform direct healings. A similar example is found in Stele 1 of the Epidaurian inscriptions. "Cleo was with child for five years." Stele 1.12 begins by saying that "Euhippus had for six years the point of a spear in his jaw."[31] In the account of Cleo's five-year pregnancy we are told that she incubated at night in the temple and after she left she gave birth to a son. The reality of the cure is indicated in the account by having the son wash himself at a fountain nearby and walk around with his mother. In the case of Euhippus, the spearhead lodged in his jaw is removed by Asclepius while he slept in the temple. The next day he left the temple a healed man; the reality of the cure was demonstrated by having Euhippus hold the spearhead in his hand as he left the temple. The regular appearance of particular literary motifs in the Epidaurian tablets is also a phenomenon occurring in the ancient miracle literature in general including the *Sacred Tales* despite the fact that the miracle story is related in numerous literary genres.

It is possible to speak of "typical" features of the miracle story, although no one miracle story in antiquity can be said to have all of the so-called typical features of the miracle story.[32] Hence, the *Sacred Tales* can be viewed as a collection of miracle stories narrated in the first-person by Aristides; likewise his religious diary can be shown to incorporate a number of typical features found in both Christian and non-Christian miracle narratives. Of course, this does not imply a historical dependence between the *Sacred Tales* and any of these other texts. These phenomenological parallels might be explained as the "logical literary consequence of a certain situation," as opposed to the "product of a certain kind of literature."[33]

---

[31] I.G.IV, 1, no. 121–122, cf. trans. Edelstein, op. cit., vol. 1, p. 229, 232.

[32] H. Van Der Loos, *The Miracles of Jesus* (Leiden, 1965), p. 120. See especially Van Der Loos' discussion of the typical features of the miracle story (p. 120).

[33] Ibid.

The Sacred Tales and Early Christian Miracle Stories

Since aretalogy is really an amorphous literary phenomenon and not a fixed literary genre, it is difficult to suppose that it had much influence in the mind of the writer in respect to the characteristics that were included in the miracle story. In order to understand the process of how a particular miracle story came to have its particular shape, it would be necessary to investigate the historical and psychological circumstances of the text's composition.[34] Our interest is merely to show some of the literary parallels between the *Sacred Tales* and other ancient texts which deal with similar subject-matter. If we turn to the New Testament, we encounter a number of interesting motifs that are found also in the *Sacred Tales*. One N.T. miracle story containing several typical motifs, many of which are also found in the *Sacred Tales*, is the story of the healing of the woman with a hemorrhage (Mark 5:25–34). The seriousness of the woman's ailment is stressed at the beginning of the story when we are told that she was ill for twelve years, and had sought out doctors who were unable to help her. Although she had spent everything she had, she still was unable to get well. Mark 5:25–26 states that "and there was a woman who had a flow of blood for twelve years, and who had suffered much under many physicians and had spent all that she had, and was no better but rather grew worse."

The "failure of the human doctors" is a regular motif in aretalogical literature, appearing both in the *Sacred Tales* and elsewhere in ancient literature. In general, Aristides stresses the seriousness of his illnesses by presenting a detailed description of his painful symptoms. He does not consistently tell us about the nature of his illnesses. Instead, he merely tells the reader about his dreams containing divine prescriptions. On some occasions, he refers to human doctors who were unable to diagnose or successfully treat his illnesses. However, the miraculous powers of Asclepius, "the true and proper doctor," (τον αληθινον προσηκοντα ιατρον), extend beyond the realm of man's capacities.

---

[34] Ibid.

In S.T.I.57 Aristides reports that after having several dreams, even the doctor realized that Asclepius' advice was far superior to his own knowledge, and so the doctor relinquished to the god. In S.T.I.61f Aristides discusses a conflict between his doctors and himself regarding the proper course of action for the treatment of a troublesome tumor. In contrast with the willingness of Theodotus, Aristides' doctor to go along with the command of Asclepius in S.T. I.57, in another passage (S.T.I.61f) Aristides' doctors stand in opposition to the paradoxical remedies prescribed by Asclepius. Once their beneficial effects are observed, the doctors no longer protest against divine medicine. This account begins with a description of the growth of a large tumor. Aristides experienced swelling, great pain and a fever for several days. His doctors recommended surgery and the ingestion of certain drugs. However, a different course of action is recommended by the god, who instead recommends that he should let the tumor grow. Following the advice of the god, Aristides incurs the criticism of his friends and yet his condition is reported to improve.

Subsequently, Aristides was ordered to perform a variety of strange acts as part of a divine therapy to promote healing. These actions included running a race unshod in the winter, riding horseback and sailing during a storm. Afterwards, his friend Zosimus told him that Asclepius had instructed him to give a certain drug to Aristides containing salt, to be rubbed on the sore spot on his body. When Aristides used this drug, his tumor vanished and his friends and doctors reacted with wonder and admiration for the providence of the god.

Similar problems are mentioned during the onset of his illnesses upon returning from Rome in 144 CE.[35] After prescribing purges to no avail, Aristides' doctors made a surgical incision from his chest to his bladder. The consequence of this procedure was unbearable pain and loss of blood. In exasperation, Aristides returns to his home in Smyrna where he encounters more doctors who are unable to help him or even diagnosis his condition. Once it is apparent that his human doctors are unable to cure him, Aristides seeks out the assistance of Asclepius. Aristides uses the warm

---

[35] S.T.II.60f.

springs nearby his home in the winter of 144 CE and there he encounters Asclepius in a dream for the first time. The first command of Asclepius is an order for Aristides to walk about barefoot, and Aristides cries out in ecstasy "Great is Asclepius" (μεγας ο Ασκληπιος).

The same phrase appears in S.T.II.22, where it is the crowd rather than Aristides who cries out the utterance. A similar type of acclamation is used by those observing a miraculous event in early Christian literature. In the Apocryphal Acts of the Apostles, a frequent response of the crowd is "Great is the God of the Christians."[36]

The "failure of the doctors" is a motif also appearing elsewhere in accounts of the miracles of Asclepius. For example, Aelian tells us about Euphronius, who was sick with pneumonia. First he sought the advice of mortal physicians. The illness did not abate. When he had reached the point of death, his friends took him to the temple of Asclepius, where he was cured by the god.[37] Even the doctor Galen knew that at Pergamum, if the god orders patients not to drink for fifteen days the patients obey, but if the same prescription is ordered by doctors, the patient will not obey.[38] Undoubtedly, the initial inability of the human doctors to cure their patients as is depicted in these stories functions as a way to underscore the miraculous nature of Asclepius' curative powers.

Scientific medicine was not completely unknown in the cult of Asclepius. Behr tells us that instances of rational medical treatment, that is, practices falling within the limits of ancient scientific medicine, appear throughout the *Sacred Tales*. However, we must be careful not to exaggerate the importance of these scientific proce-

---

[36] See Nock, *Conversion*, op. cit., p. 89; on acclamations, see Van Der Loos, op. cit., pp. 123–130.

[37] Aelian, *Fragmenta*, 89, trans. Edelstein, op. cit., vol. 1, p. 201. See also Marinus, *Vita Procli,* p. 29; Edelstein, op. cit., vol. 1, pp. 322–323; see also the account of Julian's experience, I.G., XIV, No. 966; Edelstein, op. cit., vol. 1, p. 251.

[38] Galenus, *Commentaries in Hippocratis Epidemias*, VI, IV, Sectis IV, 8; Edelstein, vol. 1, p. 202.

dures in the cult of Asclepius. Nineteenth-century rationalists studying the cult of Asclepius revealed their biases in their efforts,

> [T]o distinguish different periods of temple medicine which were characterized by different methods of healing; in pre-Roman centuries the god was supposed to have worked as the typical performer of miracles; but in the course of time he was believed to have become more rational; 'he learned medicine'; the temples themselves became sanatoria.[39]

In Roman times, the god no longer regularly performs miraculous cures when he appears in a person's dreams. In the fourth century BCE the god frequently appears in a person's dreams and performs cures, but in the Roman period, most of the cures in the cult of Asclepius involve the patient's performance of divine prescriptions which are communicated to the patient by means of allegorical dreams. Asclepius' divine prescriptions were imbued with spiritual value; frequently the temple-priests were responsible for dream interpretation, although Aristides usually interpreted his own dreams with little or no assistance from the temple priests. From the standpoint of the religious devotee, any scientific procedures that were carried out in the cult had spiritual significance. In general, any scientific therapy taking place in the cult of Asclepius occurred in a religious context.

The existence of the scientific medicine that is described in the *Sacred Tales* indicates that religion and science were not necessarily viewed as being in conflict in the minds of the members of the cult of Asclepius. However, there was a good deal of irrational medicine practiced at Pergamum, Epidaurus and elsewhere during the Roman period. In this regard, Edelstein claims that there is no indication that physicians actually played a direct role in temple healings.[40] In fact, as the above-mentioned stories of Aristides and his dealings with his doctors indicate, it appears that Asclepius' patients often enlisted the god's assistance only after the human doctors had given up any attempt to cure the individual. Behr includes

---

[39] Edelstein, op. cit., vol. II, p. 144.
[40] Ibid p. 151.

in his list of non-rational medical remedies in the *Sacred Tales* the following list: outdoor bathing and exercises being done when Aristides' health was failing him, abstinence from warm baths, strenuous summer exercises, and magic.[41]

In addition, in the above cited passage (S.T.I.61) Aristides speaks of doing many "paradoxical" things in order to obtain a cure. The word παραδοξα is used to describe various non-rational therapeutic measures performed by Aristides, such as running barefoot in the winter time, riding horse-back, etc. The term is used again in S.T.II.10 to describe his journey to Chinus which involved a difficult sea voyage, in which Asclepius predicted a shipwreck that could not be altered unless certain things were done. Aristides was instructed to leave in a skiff, overturn it in the harbor, and then be rescued and brought to the shore. In addition, Aristides was ordered to perform a purge, since the waves had stirred everything up. The contrived shipwreck was seen as Θαυμαστον to all who witnessed it. In S.T.II.24, Aristides displays narrative hesitation by asking the reader whether or not he should make a catalogue of all of his wintry, divine and strange baths. Another instance of the term παραδοξα occurs in S.T.II.47–48 where Aristides remarks about an instance involving some temple priests who confessed that they knew of no one else who had as many phlebotomies as Aristides, with a single exception of Ischron, who was one of the strange ones. However, the priests believed that Aristides surpassed even the case of Ischron apart from the other paradoxical things that happen immediately afterwards. For example, Aristides tells us that the god ordered him to draw blood from his forehead. Further, it was necessary to travel to Caicus and bathe there, after casting away some pieces of wool. The god predicted that Aristides would see a horse bathing and a temple priest named Asclepiacus by the shore. When the predictions came true, Aristides said that he experienced a comfort that was difficult for anyone except a god to comprehend, and certainly difficult for a man to write about. Weinreich views this paradoxical element as a typical feature of the

---

[41] Behr, op. cit., p. 37.

miracle story. To illustrate his point, Weinreich mentions several texts including the *Sacred Tales* and Marinos' *Vita Procli* 31.[42]

The word παραδοξα occurs in one of Jesus' many healing miracles, Luke 5:26.[43] Following the healing of a palsied man, the account concludes with a description of the amazement of those witnessing the miracle where the term appears again. Another typical feature of the miracle story is the suddenness of the miracle. Terms such as ταχυ and αυτημαρ are sometimes used.[44] Thus, in Mark 5:25f the woman with the hemorrhage touched the robe of Jesus and her hemorrhage instantly stopped bleeding.[45] For the most part, Aristides is vague with respect to the time involved in the various healings in the *Sacred Tales*. In some cases, the benefits resulting from the performance of the divine prescriptions were not felt immediately. Yet an example can be cited where healing took place quickly.[46] Furthermore, the so-called motif of the "proof of the reality of the cure" is not formally present in the *Sacred Tales*.

In respect to the technique of the miracle-worker and his treatment of the sick, it is often the case that the miracle-worker stands over the sick person as he engages in the healing process.[47] In S.T.II.18 Asclepius delivers one of his many divine proclamations to Aristides while standing in front of Aristides' bed. While lying in bed with a terrible fever, Aristides saw Athena standing before him making soothing utterances.[48] Frequently in the healing miracle, certain authoritative pronouncements are made by the miracle-worker. In Matt 9:2 Jesus addresses the sick with the term

---

[42] Weinreich, *Antike Heilungswunder*, op. cit., pp. 198–199.

[43] Cf. *Aelius Aristides and the New Testament*, ed. P. W. Van der Horst, (Leiden, 1980), p. 23.

[44] See Plutarch, *Perikles*, 13; Athena is described as follows: ταχυ και ραδιως ιασατο τον ανΘρωπον. Cf. Weinreich, op. cit., p. 197.

[45] See Van Der Loos' discussion of this motif; op. cit., p. 126f; an example of this typical feature appears in the writings of Quintus Smyraneus, *Posthomerica*, IV, 396–404 in Edelstein, op. cit., vol. 1, p. 96.

[46] See Matt 5:40; Edelstein, op. cit., vol. 1, p. 230.

[47] Luke 4:39; Asclepius cured Theopompos "by approaching the sick man's bed and holding out to him his healing hand." Weinreich, *Antike Heilungswunder*, op. cit., p. 1; see also Lucian, *Philops*, op. cit., 16.

[48] S.T.II.41.

Θαρσει or "Take courage." Asclepius informs Aristides in a dream that it would be efficacious to recite certain phrases, including φυλαξον or "take care."[49]

A regular feature of the miracle story involves the god ordering a devotee to make a record of the miracles occurring in his life. In S.T.II.2 we learn that Asclepius ordered Aristides to copy down his dreams. In the ancient world, the dream often functioned as a means through which a god might request an individual to perform certain actions, such as to build a temple dedicated to a particular god, make a sacrifice to the gods, or to compose a literary composition dedicated to a god.[50] As Oppenheim writes,

> in their desire to stress the supernatural origin and hence the validity and the value of literary products, authors and compilers alike have often made use of the dream as the alleged medium through which a specific opus was communicated to them.[51]

Similar to Aristides, many patients, including Marius and Julius Apellas of Idrias, were ordered by Asclepius to make a record of benefits conferred upon them by the god.[52] Likewise, in the text in honor of the god Imouthes who is identified with Asclepius, the god orders a devotee to write a literary composition about the god's miraculous intervention. The unknown author of the *Oxy. Pap.* 1382 shares in common with Lucius and Aristides a difficulty in describing the mighty deeds of the god; the author states that this literary task really should be assigned to the gods rather than mortals.[53] The author's vision occurred while he was experiencing an intense pain in his side and he had a fever which had induced a

---

[49] Ibid., I.71.

[50] See E. R. Dodds, *The Greeks and the Irrational*, p. 108, n. 30, 31, 32, 22; Oppenheim, *The Interpretation of Dreams in the Ancient Near East*, (Transactions of the American Philosophical Society, (Philadelphia, 1956), p. 192f.

[51] Oppenheim, op. cit., p. 193.

[52] Appellas' testimony appears in Mary Hamilton's *Incubation*, (Londres, 1906), p. 40; also see *Revue Archelogie* trans. S. Reinach, vol. II, (1883), p. 295

[53] *Oxy. Pap.* 1382, vol. ii., lines 40–42.

state of semi-consciousness. His mother was standing next to him, and suddenly she had a vision of a god who was clothed in shining raiment and carrying a book in his left hand. Once the god vanished, she wished to declare the "virtues of the god" (αρετην Θεου), but everything she saw had already appeared to her son in a dream. Following this, the author discusses the problems related to the god's command to compose a book by stating,

> I was at a loss and with difficulty, since I disparaged it, felt the divine obligation of the composition... I was neglecting the divine book, invoking thy providence and was filled with thy divinity, I hastened to the inspired task of the history...[54]

Initially, Aristides recoiled from the task of recording his story, yet eventually the power of the god enabled him to discuss his experiences based upon his old notes. Festugiere views Aristides' comment in S.T.II as an instance of the well-known motif in Hellenistic religious literature in which a devotee receives an order from the god to narrate his dreams or to write a book in the god's honor. This task poses large difficulties yet the god inspires the devotee to perform the task.[55]

In summary, we have noted several typical motifs found in aretalogy and have noted their presence in the *Sacred Tales*. The text also contains many terms that are present in ancient miracle literature. In general, we may conclude that the *Sacred Tales* exhibits many of the structural components of aretalogical literature. However, on one level of abstraction, some traits are particular instances of universal religious structures characterizing the phenomenology of religious experience; for example, the motif of "the difficulty of describing the works of the god" might be classified as an example of the ineffability of religious experience. The presence of light (φως) in divine epiphanies is a universal religious phenomenon. Aristides' religious experience is not entirely unique, but rather has elements found elsewhere in his cultural milieu; it cannot be properly apprehended if our analysis limits itself to comparing the

---

[54] *Oxy. Pap.* 1382, trans. Grenfell and Hunt, op. cit., p. 231.
[55] A. J. Festugiere, *Etudes d'Histoire et de Philogie*, op. cit., p. 92.

Sacred Tales to other testimony coming from the cult of Asclepius alone. An adequate historical interpretation cannot avoid understanding Aristides' religious experience in the context of the general interest of many in Late Antiquity in divine revelation, salvation and the telling of miracles.

CHAPTER FIVE: ARISTIDES AND THE RELIGIOUS CLIMATE OF LATE ANTIQUITY

TRUE BELIEVERS IN THE GRECO-ROMAN WORLD

This chapter situates Aristides' piety against the background of the prominent religious attitudes held by the ancients concerning the miraculous and supernatural phenomena. Our primary interest will be to ascertain the extent to which Aristides' acceptance of the reality of miracles and dream epiphanies should be considered as normative or representative of the popular spiritual trends of his era. Obviously, there were many in the second century who had a skeptical attitude in regards to the veracity of the reports of supernatural events circulating in the world. However, there were others who could be characterized as somewhat naïve in their unquestioned acceptance of such alleged miraculous occurrences. Aristides could be classified as one of the more credulous individuals living in the Greco-Roman world.

There are a number of ancient writers, especially in the realm of ancient fiction, who provide us with good sources of information about many of the popular superstitions of the era. Given the fact that the *Sacred Tales* is an autobiographical document, it does not mean that it has nothing in common, at least stylistically, with some of the fictional works of the era. Some modern commentators have noted that Aristides' descriptions of external reality—including his journeys between temples and various anecdotes about his life in the temple precincts—reflect a style that has a remarkably picturesque quality to it and is vividly realistic. This stylistic trait is also found in the ancient novel and Hellenistic stories of magic. As Reardon states, the *Sacred Tales* and the ancient novel share a thematic interest in the life of the individual and his religious relationship with the gods.[1]

On a macroscopic level, the central theme of the Hellenistic era beginning from the time of Alexander the Great is the rise of individualism, and the interest in individual salvation. Specifically, in the second century CE,

> the entire culture, pagan as well as Christian, was moving into a phase in which religion was to be coexistent with life, and the quest for God was to cast its shadow over all other human activities.[2]

The religious trends in this historical period suggest varying degrees of credulity and belief in occult forces which are reflected in much of the extant literature. We should note Robert Grant's shrewd insight that "the credulity of the Greeks and Romans has often been exaggerated in modern times."[3] In ancient times, as in any historical period, different individuals and groups display differing degrees of credulity. Although Grant notes that credulity was perhaps at its lowest ebb during the late Hellenistic age, a shift towards religious faith and superstition begins to occur at the end of the first century BCE. Among the Neopythagoreans there was a marked interest in the marvelous. For example, Alexander Polyhistor wrote a *Collection of Marvels*. In the second century CE Philostratus wrote his romance on the religious figure Apollonius of Tyana. In the second century CE Phlegon's work entitled *On Marvels* was composed, which included a collection of ghost stories, tales of hermaphrodites, stories of the discovery of large bones and myths of centaurs. There is ample evidence to show that the masses were turning in great eagerness to new cults and philosophies and were especially interested in esoteric knowledge. For example, in *Alexander the Quack Prophet* Lucian presents a humorous story of a phony holy man named Alexander and his cult which he founded in

---

[1] B. P. Reardon, *Courants Litteraire Grecs Des II et III Siecles Apres J-C*, (Paris, 1971), p. 263.

[2] Dodds, *Pagan and Christian in an Age of Anxiety*, op. cit., p. 101.

[3] Robert Grant, *Miracles and Natural Law*, (Amsterdam, 1952), p. 41.

Abonoteichus, near the Black Sea.[4] Alexander's teacher was Apollonius of Tyana.

In distinction to Aristides, there are many examples of "holy men" in the ancient Mediterranean world. Although Aristides is quite aware of the divine quality of his dreams and interprets them in such a fashion, we should note that even he was not enamored of his religious experience to the point of becoming a charismatic "holy man." However, there are numerous individuals such as Apollonius of Tyana and Alexander of Abonoteichus who qualify as examples of the *theos aner*. In each of these cases, the divine man is responsible for performing miraculous healings and other uncanny feats, yet in the case of Aelius Aristides he is never the source of his healings nor does he present himself in such terms. He merely is the recipient and benefactor of the many blessing of Asclepius. Rather than performing any miracles, he is merely the receiver of the many divine healings. Aristides is a religious man not a "divine man."

If we compare the life of a *theos aner* to the life of Aristides, it is apparent that neither is Aristides a charlatan nor a performer of miracles. One such example of a *theos aner* is presented in the humorous story *Alexander the Quack Prophet*. As a young man, Alexander together with a friend, decided to masquerade as magicians for their mutual prophet. At one point they realized that many were willing to pay gold in order to obtain knowledge of the future. Hence, these two decided to create an oracle. The oracle was to be located in Abonoteichus, since according to Alexander the people of the area were,

> superstitious and well-heeled-yokels for the most part… all a man had to do was come along at his heels someone tootling a flute or beating a drum or clashing cymbals, and offer to tell fortunes with a sieve as the saying goes, and the next minute all their jaws would drop and they'd stare at him like a god from heaven.[5]

---

[4] Cf. Lucian, "Alexander the Quack Prophet" in *Selected Satires of Lucian*, ed. and trans., Lionel Casson, (New York, 1962), pp. 267–299.
[5] Ibid., p. 273.

Upon arriving in town, Alexander acted as if he were a celebrity and even pretended to be frothing at the mouth in order to attract naive spectators. Not only was Alexander able to gull the inhabitants of Abonoteichus with his quackery, but soon many from neighboring locations such as Bithynia, Galatia and Thrace came to the oracle.

Although the text is an excellent piece of creative writing, it is not wholly fictitious; undoubtedly there was such an actual cult situated in Abonoteichus, and this is evidenced by the existence of coins bearing the image of the snake god Glycon which is associated with the cult of Asclepius.[6] In spite of Lucian's satirical intentions, this text offers us a penetrating glance at the credulous world of Asia Minor in the second century CE.

Credulity was not merely found among the lower levels of Greco-Roman society. There were many others among the Roman upper class who shared Aristides' heightened concern with matters of religion and health. A good example of this concern among the upper classes of Roman society is expressed in the correspondence of M. Cornelius Fronto.[7] Fronto was one of the prominent figures of the Second Sophistic. Many of the letters were written to or received from Marcus Aurelius and frequently the subject-matter of the letters was decidedly religious. As Liebeschuetz points out in his discussions of the letters, Fronto's belief in the powers of Tyche are expressed when he claims that human life is controlled by the gods.[8] Likewise, similar sentiments are expressed by the emperor Marcus. Thus, we read "if the gods allow it, we have some hope of recovery."[9] Fronto states that "I propose—with divine agreement—to take a drive tomorrow."[10] Many of the letters consist of

---

[6] Ibid., p. 268.

[7] *The Correspondence of Marcus Cornelius Fronto*, ed. and trans. C. R. Haines, 2 vols., (Cambridge, Mass, 1957); see also Dorothy M. Brock, *Studies in Fronto and His Age,* (Cambridge, England, 1911).

[8] J. H. W. G. Liebeschuets, *Continuity and Change in Roman Religion*, (London, 1979), pp. 205–206.

[9] Ibid., p. 206, n. 1 IV II from Marcus Aurelius ed. C. R. Haines, 1.202; cf. Ibid., v. 55, M. Aurelius to Fronto Haines, 1.252.

[10] Ibid., p. 206 n. 5, Ibid., 40 (Fronto to M. Aurelius)-Haines 1.242.

long discussions regarding Fronto's various illnesses and his dependence on the gods for assistance.

SKEPTICS AND DOUBTERS IN ANCIENT TIMES

Of course, not everyone in antiquity believed in miracles, tales of the incredible and so forth. There were many skeptics as well. One of the most famous of all the skeptics of antiquity is Cicero, who discusses his ideas on dreams and dreams interpretation in *De Divinatione* I, xxf.[11] In this text, Cicero speaks about Chrysippus and Antipater, each of whom wrote a treatise on dreams. Chrysippus interprets dreams according to certain principles set forth by Antiphon. Quintus, Cicero's brother, states that the literary dreams presented in Ennius' *Annales* are poetic fictions, even though their form does not differ greatly from real dreams. Quintus refers to these types of dreams as "myths." In Book II Cicero presents his criticisms about those who believe in the revelatory power of dream visions. Dreams are compared to the hallucinations of drunken persons and the insane. Cicero states that since the visions of the former persons are invalid, why would anyone trust the reliability of dream visions as a source of truth about spiritual matters? Again Cicero favors putting trust in scientific explanation as opposed to the advice of "fortune-telling hags." As to the accuracy of men's ability to recall their dreams, Cicero believes it is impossible to remember the countless and constantly changing series of dreams experienced by an individual or to observe and to write down the subsequent results.

Lucian vigorously attacked the "deceivers of antiquity," including writers such as Homer and Herodotus. In his *True History* he sets out to write a satirical essay imitating and making allusions to what he considers to be the fabulous tall tales and lies told by eminent poets, philosophers, and historians from ancient times. According to Lucian "the arch-exponent of, and model for, this sort of tomfoolery, is Homer's Odysseus telling the court of Alcinous about a bag with the winds in it, one-eyed giants, cannibals,

---

[11] Cicero, *De Divinatione*, I, XXf, trans. William Armistead Falconer, Loeb Classical Library, (London and New York, 1923).

savages, even many-headed monsters and magic drugs that change shipmates into swine..."[12] Interestingly enough, when Aristides begins his account of how he becomes involved in the cult of Asclepius for the first time, his trip to Rome and the onset of his many illnesses, he compares his story to the tale told to Alcinous by Odysseus.[13]

It is often difficult to determine just how credulous or skeptical a particular writer is with respect to religious matters. Between the poles of complete gullibility and radical doubt lies a middle ground. For example, Maximus of Tyre, on the one hand, expresses his belief that Asclepius can appear in his waking consciousness, yet he also states that it is hard to have faith in the portrayal of the gods offered by the poets and these therefore should be interpreted in an allegorical way.[14]

The classical philosopher Aristotle presents his views regarding the nature of dreams in two essays entitled *De Somniis* and *De Divinatione Per Somnum*. Aristotle takes a middle position with respect to divinatory dreams by stating that he can neither dismiss them nor put his confidence in their reliability.[15] Aristotle does not doubt that some men are capable of receiving prophetic dreams, although most of these dreams are really the results of "mere coincidences." Similar to Artemidorus, Aristotle refuses to grant the possibility that a deity sends these dreams to humanity. That a god does not send dreams is shown by the simple fact that prophetic dreams, vivid dreams, and so forth occur primarily in the dream life of individuals of an inferior type. Uneducated persons are receptive to seeing the future, since their minds are empty; the deranged have foresight since their normal mental activity does not hinder the

---

[12] Lucius, "A True Story," in *Selected Satires of Lucian*, ed. and trans by Lionel Casson, (New York, 1962), pp. 14–15

[13] S.T.II.60; other satires were written by Lucian that are relevant to our discussion; cf. *Selected Satires of Lucian*, ed. and trans. Lionel Casson, op. cit.

[14] Maximus, Diss. X.I, III; XXXVIII cf. Grant, *Miracles and Natural Law*, op. cit., p. 69.

[15] Aristotle, *De Divinatione Per Somnum*, 462b.

alien movements. Hence, the deranged generally have a keen perception of the future.[16]

SYSTEMS OF DREAM INTERPRETATION IN THE SACRED TALES AND ELSEWHERE

Many ancients believed that dreams were a potential source of knowledge about the future; furthermore, many claimed that the gods revealed themselves in dreams. Of course, not all dreams were revelatory and as a result there arose a need to devise a set of principles to distinguish between significant and non-significant dreams.

Artemidorus' *Oneirocritica* is the only ancient treatise on dream-interpretation that is extant. Fortunately, it presents a good deal of information about dream-interpretation in Greek society.[17] According to one modern commentator on this second century CE text, the major element of this text "is its rational, practical approach" since Artemidorus deals with dreams "in a logical, seemingly scientific way."[18] Artemidorus' general motive for writing the *Oneirocritica* was an attempt to combat "those who are trying to do away with divination."[19] In his system of dream-interpretation, Artemidorus defines *oneiros* as a dream showing the future state of things. Even though his religio-philosophical outlook includes an acceptance of the existence of prophetic dreams, Artemidorus shows little interest in whether or not a dream is sent from the gods. Moreover, he demonstrates his skepticism when he states that it is obvious that many of the divine prescriptions dealing with medical matters recorded by various people are absolutely ridiculous. He states that it

---

[16] Ibid., 464a.

[17] See White's translation, (Park Ridge, New Jersey, 1975).

[18] Artemidorus, *The Interpretation of Dreams,* trans, Robert White, op. cit., p. 7. Another scholar, Reardon, claims that although Artemidorus intended to write a work based on empirical observation of the dreams of other people, still many of his ideas are not scientific at all. Therefore the text should be regarded as 'pseudo-scientific' work. Reardon, pp. 242–254.

[19] Artemidorus, *The Interpretation of Dreams*, trans. Robert J. White, op. cit., p. 13.

is plain to any rational person that such prescriptions are the product of literary invention. Hence he writes,

> And so when they write such as this, it seems to me that they are demonstrating a mentality that is better equipped to mold dreams than to comprehend the love that the gods feel towards men. For not a single example of a dream that is actually like this has come to us...[20]

Having reviewed the varying attitudes towards the supernatural existing in the Hellenistic world, we are in a better position to situate Aristides' religious orientation towards his dreams. When viewed against the background of the various ancient attitudes about dreams including the views of Cicero, Aristotle and Artemidorus, Aristides should be classified among the more religiously-inclined individuals of his era. Unlike Artemidorus, Aristides generally avoids any elaborate de-codification of ambiguous dream symbols.[21] Thus, in S.T.I.7 the experience of being befouled is interpreted to mean that it is necessary to bathe. Often long, complex symbolic dreams are given a simple and direct interpretation, based on information presented at the end of the dream.[22] Sometimes, as in S.T.I.33, a dream is so vivid that there is no need for any interpretation. In other cases, an interpretation of dream symbols actually occurs in the dream itself. In one instance, Aristides dreamed that he saw a great ditch dug and witnessed quantities of dirt being carried out. In the morning he interpreted the dream to mean that

---

[20] Ibid., p. 195.

[21] Behr states "in interpreting his dreams, no matter how much symbolism they may contain, Aristides shows a marked bias toward treating only their direct and clear implications." As Behr notes, Aristides interpreted dream symbols either pragmatically or theoretically; in the former "he inferred the dreams significance and acted accordingly;" and in the latter the dream symbol "became clear to him empirically after the dream had fulfilled itself." Behr, op. cit., pp. 193–194.

[22] Cf. S.T. I.17–21, I.22, I.36–40, I.42–45. In S.T. I.54–55 he derives a simple medical prescription such as fasting or bathing from a series of complex imagery. Behr compares Aristides with other dream interpreters, especially Artemidorus; cf. Behr, op. cit., appendix, p. 193f.

he should take an enema.²³ Such a common sense interpretation of this dream varies greatly from the subtle hermeneutic of dreams presented by Artemidorus.

In his commentary, Behr outlines some of the general features of ancient dream interpretation. He states that in antiquity there was a general belief that "the soul of the dreamer... portrayed all dreams. For many, including Aristides, the soul was only an intermediary and received its dreams from a divine source."²⁴ Furthermore, Behr notes that Plato traced the cause of non-predictive dreams back to disorderly bodily states; predictive dreams resulted from the agency of daemons who transmitted dreams to the dreamer's soul.²⁵ According to Behr, this two-fold system of dream-interpretation found in Plato continued to exist in the works of Artemidorus, Iamblichus and Synesius. Growing out of the two-fold system, a three-fold system develops. The third category of dreams was the dream-oracle; the dream oracle is a dream that is sent by the gods as opposed to daemons. Behr claims that Aristides was aware of the latter system since he uses terms such as χρησμος, χρησμωδια and λογια. Artemidorus follows Plato in distinguishing between predictive and non-predictive dreams. Whereas Artemidorus stresses the importance of viewing the total gestalt of the dream, Aristides does not concern himself with the overall sense of the dream when he interprets it. Although there are few parallelisms existing between the *Oneirocritica* and the *Sacred Tales*, there are an overwhelming number of differences between them. It is very unlikely that Aristides depended upon Artemidorus in writing the *Sacred Tales*, even though he had vague familiarity with traditional systems of dream interpretation.²⁶

---

²³ S.T.I.46.
²⁴ Behr, op. cit., p. 172.
²⁵ Plato, Repub., 571C–572B.
²⁶ Cf. Behr, op. cit., p. 196. "The bias which led Aristides to stress the clarity of the medical dream caused him to suppress the symbolic content of his dreams so that direct parallelisms between the detail in Artemidorus and any stated interpretations in Aristides' dreams is very rare." Since Aristides wrote his treatise thirty years before Aristides wrote the *Sacred Tales*, it is impossible that Artemidorus was influenced by Aristides' dream diary.

Certainly Aristides would remain a very religious and credulous individual regardless of the historical era in which lived. On the other hand, his obsession with his dreams as well as his interest in Asclepius' miraculous interventions in his life cannot be entirely separated from its historical context, namely, the growing religious revival developing throughout the Roman Empire beginning sometime in the first century BCE. Robert Grant points out that,

> in the first century BCE the foundations for the later revival of credulity were being laid... we see in the first century an increase in interest in astrology, magic and a credulous Pythagoreanism.[27]

The difference between the religious climate of the second century CE and the next two centuries is essentially one of degree. In assessing the contents of the *Sacred Tales*, it is rather obvious that we are dealing with a kind of exaggerated spirituality. In spite of the fact that the second-century Greco-Roman world could be characterized as a time of heightened concern among the masses with religio-magical ideas and practices as well as growing interest in eastern religious cults, it is equally important to realize that many of the conclusions about Aristides' piety generally would not apply to the average person living in Greco-Roman times nor any other historical period for that matter. In his case we are dealing with a special class of individual, namely, *homo religiosus*, and as such many of the typical traits of religious behavior have become intensified.

Aristides' piety and its literary expression in the *Sacred Tales* incorporate numerous traits present in the religious culture of Greco-Roman times. This does not mean that his piety can be explained solely as an embodiment of the common core of religious values, attitudes, and themes of his era, since it is also conditioned by his own unique personal psychological disposition. On the other hand, his religious visions and other ecstatic experiences were not solely an expression of his private neurosis. Surely, such an argument is patently reductionistic as well as fallacious. Aristides' religious experience is not entirely typical but it certainly reflects elements of

---

[27] Grant, *Miracle and Natural Law in Graeco-Roman and Early Christian Thought*, op. cit., p. 61.

his personality and it also reflects elements within the social environment of the Hellenistic world. In Chapter Eight we will take a closer look at the psychological dimension of Aristides' religiosity.

Part Two: Psychological Considerations

Chapter Six: Analysis of the Manifest Contents of Aristides' Dreams

The Manifest Contents of Aristides' Dreams

In previous chapters we have discussed numerous literary and cultural influences upon the *Sacred Tales*. In discussing self-portrayal in antiquity, we have observed a peculiar reticence on the part of the Greeks and Romans to openly discuss their inner life. Unlike modern autobiographers, the literary intentions of an ancient autobiographer did not include a desire to present a "history of the soul." Undoubtedly, Aristides inherited this viewpoint from the ancient autobiographical tradition. Aristides' somewhat careless, ahistorical portrayal of his own life reflects the influence of particular conventions of language and attitudes towards self-expression present in ancient society. However, in the case of Aristides there is a conspicuous absence of the "introspective conscience" unlike that which characterizes later Christian autobiographers such as Augustine. Aristides is no "sick soul," unlike his Christian counterparts.

A number of parallels have been identified between the dreams and visions of the *Sacred Tales* and analogous types of visionary experiences recorded by a number of other individuals living in Greco-Roman times. Furthermore, many features of the healing miracles present in the *Sacred Tales* are also found in other documents belonging to the tradition of ancient miracle literature. It is very unlikely that Aristides was familiar with any of the previously discussed miracle stories. However, since Aristides was deeply involved in the cult of Asclepius for seventeen years of his life, there is good reason to believe that he had a general familiarity with various conventions associated with the reporting of miracles and visions in antiquity.

In describing his religious experiences, Aristides unconsciously incorporates many of the elements present in the visionary literature and miracle texts of his times. Unfortunately, there is no documentary evidence pertaining to Aristides' familiarity with the rules and conventions associated with ancient miracle and dream literature. Even at the level of conscious awareness itself, it is possible that Aristides' dream-visions incorporated many of the traits found in these literary genres.

The present chapter conducts a psychological examination of Aristides' religious experience by examining the manifest contents of his dreams, that is, the actual dream images and symbols (the conscious/pre-conscious level) as they appear in the *Sacred Tales*. In the next chapter we will examine the latent meaning of many of these same dreams (the unconscious level). This distinction between the manifest and latent contents of dreams was first proposed by Sigmund Freud in his monumental work *The Interpretation of Dreams*. A chief concern will be to identify the predominant patterns and typical themes of his dream life as they appear at the level pre-conscious and conscious level of experience. This will serve as our starting point for an exploration of Aristides' unconscious life. Our analysis of the approximately one hundred and thirty dreams recorded in the text will include an investigation into the extent to which the divine epiphanies recorded therein contain certain "typical features" of the dream epiphany of the god which also appear in ancient dream literature. Furthermore, we shall examine some of the categories of dream interpretation employed by Aristides and situate these principles of dream interpretation in the sociohistorical context.

ANTHROPOLOGICAL APPROACHES TO THE DREAM

In recent times, anthropologists have become interested in utilizing methods employed by psychologists and psychiatrists for studying personality. Such an interest has grown out of a concern among anthropologists for understanding the culture-personality dynamic.[1]

---

[1] cf. Milton Singer, "A Survey of Culture and Personality; Theory and Research," *Studying Personality Cross-Culturally*, ed. Bert Kaplan, (Evanston, Illinois and Elmsford, New York, 1961), p. 551.

Similar concerns are shared by students of the historical sciences. Given this anthropological interest in culture/personality matters, there has been an interest in developing a suitable conceptual schema designed to describe and explain in an unbiased fashion the data gathered regarding how culture impacts personality.[2]

For the purposes of this study we are interested in appropriating some of the methods used in cross-cultural dream research. The anthropologist Dorothy Eggan has noted that little attention has been directed to the dream—"that most profoundly subjective of all personality productions—to further these ends."[3] What has intrigued Eggan and others is the systematic study and analysis of the manifest content of dreams coming from primitive culture as a means of expanding our knowledge about the role of culture in personality development.[4] In her anthropological dream research, Eggan has developed a methodology for identifying patterns and structural relationships in the dream world of the individual. The essential feature of this research method involves an assessment of the relative numerical frequency of particular dream-images as they appear in the manifest content of the dreams of a Hopi Indian. By means of tabulating the frequency of dream images in a person's dream life, the goal is to discover dream patterns and correlate them to individual personality traits and issues.

---

[2] Dorothy Eggan, "Dream Analysis," *Studying Personality Cross-Culturally*, op. cit. p. 551.

[3] Ibid. While discussing his Walapai studies Kroeber writes "I had the impression that the dreams revealed more personality than the life-histories… a dream is bound to be personal, while a life-history can be heavily depersonalized." A. Kroeber, "A Southwestern Personality Type," *The Nature of Culture*, (Chicago, Ill., 1952) p. 324, cited by Eggan op. cit. p. 552.

[4] Cf., Dorothy Eggan, "The Manifest Content of Dreams: A Challenge to Social Science," *American Anthropologist*, vol. 54, no. 4, (1954), pp. 461–485.

APPLYING A QUANTITATIVE APPROACH TO THE DREAMS OF ARISTIDES

If Eggan's approach is suitable for the study of the manifest contents of the dreams of individuals living in different cultures, then there is no reason to believe that it cannot be applicable for studying the dreams of individuals living in different historical eras. Applying this method to the dreams of Aristides yields some interesting results. There is a prevalence of medical and religious images as well as rhetorical themes, and material dealing with temple life and incubation, etc. On the surface, most of the dreams recorded in the text consist of imagery derived from Aristides' conscious experience occurring in the waking state.

Modern dream researchers focus on the importance of our daily waking experiences in our dream life. The majority of our dreams are made up of images, themes and people who exist in our waking life. Currently, in the field of dream research, there are many who are interested in exploring the so-called "continuity hypothesis", that is, the connection between our conscious waking experiences and our dreams. Theoretically speaking, the scope of the continuity hypothesis should extend to the dreams of ancient individuals such as Aristides and St Perpetua who lived outside the boundaries of the modern era. In fact, many of Aristides' dreams reflect identifiable continuities with his day-to-day waking consciousness.[5]

Aristides' dreams vary in length from brief casual remarks of a few words to several paragraphs. On occasion, Aristides merely alludes to a particular dream without offering any detailed information about its contents. Frequently, Aristides groups together in his narrative dream episodes that are closely related in terms of their occurrence as well as their thematic content.[6] The word

---

[5] Domhoff, William, *Finding Meaning in Dreams: A Quantitative Approach*, (New York, 1996).

[6] Behr states that "unlike Artemidorus, Aristides did not descry a unity within his dreams which are faithfully reproduced not always as great single dreams but as a multiple series of different subjects or a progression of related vignettes." Behr, op. cit., p. 193; cf. S.T. I.17–21, I.24–26, II.40–42, III.3–4, IV.38–42, V.57–66. Instead of viewing the series of

υστερον or "later" is used to link one dream episode with the next in these series of dream-visions. This vague word υστερον introduces a dreamlike quality into the text, since in the surrealistic world of dreams temporality is not strongly felt. Aristides also uses the phrase μετα ταυτα ("after that") when introducing a new dream account. Likewise, he often mentions seeing one thing or being in one place and at the same time somehow (αμα πως) seeing another thing or being in another place.[7] Again, such phrases underscore the dreamlike quality of the narrative and indicate that we are dealing with an authentic dream narrative.

In those dreams of Aristides which do not have epiphanies of the gods, mortals often appear in the scenario. Aristides' friends, such as Zosimus, appear in his dreams along with his servants, his foster fathers, fellow orators, government officials, temple priests, and doctors, all of whom play a significant role in his waking life. Usually, Aristides' "narcissistic" dreams involve the receipt of praise for his rhetorical accomplishments; these dreams are heavily populated with various prestigious figures such as emperors, especially Antoninus, as well as foreign rulers such as Volgases.

Aristides occupied a prominent position in his society and regularly dealt with Roman emperors and other political figures of the day. Hence, their appearance in Aristides' dreams is not really surprising or necessarily indicative of a narcissistic personality. Instead they are simply fanciful reflections of events occurring in his waking life. Not only does Aristides receive praise in his dreams from politicians, but he is also lauded by archetypal literary figures such as Plato and Sophocles who occupy a central place in his mind as models of professionalism. There is a preponderance of male figures and few females throughout the narrative.

---

dream episodes as belonging to a larger dream, Aristides distinguishes each episode as distinct. It is likely that these series of dream visions occurred on the same night. See also Dodds, *Pagan and Christian in An Age of Anxiety*, op. cit., p. 41.

[7] Behr writes, "the innumerable uses of 'somehow' or 'at the same time' indicate Aristides was just as incapable of verbalizing his dreams to conform to the requirements of reason as all men are." Behr, op. cit., p. 117; cf. S.T.III.21, V23.

The most prominent figure in Aristides' dreams, other than himself, of course, is the god Asclepius. A few other deities, including Isis, Athena, Sarapis, and Telesphorus also make infrequent appearances. Asclepius functions primarily as an authority figure in Aristides' dreams, since he regularly gives commands and advice concerning Aristides' life, especially regarding medical and therapeutic matters. Other deities, and even mortals, also serve in this capacity, especially Zosimus, his close companion, and various unidentified priests, doctors, and acquaintances. A persistent image in his preconscious mind is the image of bathing, which is discussed profusely in the text.

Particular attention should be paid to any emotional response occurring in the dream state, since this factor weighs heavily in assessing the overall psychological profile of the individual. We would expect to find a healthy individual's dreams emitting more positive than negative emotional responses. In the case of Aristides, there are a disproportionately greater number of positive emotional responses in comparison to negative emotional responses. Such a state of affairs serves as one explanation why Aristides enjoyed recalling and re-telling many of his dreams. Furthermore, it strongly suggests that many commentators of the *Sacred Tales* are wrong; Aristides' psychic constitution was not as pathological as past commentators have suggested. Most of Aristides' positive emotional responses occur in the context of religious experience and include feelings of religious happiness, wonder, and joy. Positive emotions are also expressed in connection with worship, prayer and the consolation of grief over the death of his companion Zosimus. On the negative side, Aristides records a few anxiety dreams involving feelings of distress. Usually, these dreams feature Aristides being chased, attacked, or persecuted by various hostile forces. Undoubtedly, these dreams have latent significance, which will be discussed in Chapter Eight. The existence of anxiety-type dreams in the *Sacred Tales* is, however, another good indication that we are dealing with a genuine record of Aristides' dreams. Analogous types of dreams involving anxiety, being chased by hostile forces, and the like are regularly experienced by many.[8] Even Homer has something to say concerning being chased in a dream, for he writes, "As in a dream a man is not able to follow one who runs from him, nor can the runner escape, nor the other pursue him…"[9]

Physical pain and discomfort are reported in Aristides' dreams more frequently than feelings of physical pleasure, which can be explained by virtue of the fact that in his waking experience physical pain as opposed to pleasure was a more conspicuous element. Another theme in his dreams involves Aristides being situated in a dangerous place where there is a potential threat of harm to his physical well-being.

Other images also appear in his dreams, although they are far too numerous to catalogue. Numerous references are made to ladders, animals, food, astronomical phenomena, etc. In some dreams, Aristides travels abroad, but most of the dreams present Aristides in the context of the surroundings of the temple, the countryside near his home, or in the home.

The following chart presents the evidence regarding the numerical frequency of selected dream-images as they appear in the *Sacred Tales*. A numerical approach to the manifest-content of Aristides' dreams enables the investigator to objectively assess the relative frequency of particular dream-images in the text, as well as to observe significant relationships and patterns in the dream life of Aristides.[10]

---

[8] For some clinical parallels to Aristides' anxiety dreams and a general discussion of the subject see S. Freud, *The Interpretation of Dreams*, 3rd edition, trans. and ed. James Strachey, (New York, 1955), p. 267f. With respect to the healthy side of Aristides' personality, we should keep in mind Devereux' comment that "psychoanalysis is interested in transforming the 'bad' into the 'good.' It is more interested in sublimation than in neurosis." Devereux, *Dreams in Greek Tragedy*, (Berkeley and Los Angeles) 1976, p. XIX.

[9] Homer, *Iliad*, 22, 199–200, cf. *Gospel of Truth*, 29–30.

[10] The idea for such a chart was suggested by the work of the anthropologist Dorothy Eggan in her article "The Manifest Content of Dreams: A Challenge to Social Sciences," op. cit. pp. 461–485.

FREQUENCY OF DREAM IMAGES IN THE SACRED TALES

friends	8	boys	2
Zosimus	5	Athenians	1
servants	12	foster brother	1
foster fathers	6	foreigners	2
emperor	1	Government and political officials	2
Rosander the philosopher	1	Rufinus	1
Plato	1	temple priests	5
orators	5	temple servants	1
Herodorus the poet	1	children	1
Sophocles	1	Aristides' teachers	2
young men	3	Aristides' doctors	7
		Nurses	2

Total: 88

Positive		Negative	
feeling of relief	2	anxiety	2
being pleased	3	anger	3
greeting a friend	1	distrust	1
gladness	1	distress	3
marvelous feeling	5	fear	1
praising the god	4	feeling of annoyance	2
prayer	3	*Total:*	*12*
the god jokes	1		
feeling of religious wonder	7		
worship of a statue	1		
joy	4		
consolation of grief	2		
Total:	*33*		

Praise for Aristides	14
Feeling of physical pleasure	1
Physical hazard	
accidents, danger	11
violence	1
attack, persecution	3
Total:	*15*

Physical pain and discomfort		6
Divine epiphanies		
Asclepius		5
Athena		1
Sarapis		2
Phoebus Apollo		1
Isis		1
Hermes		1
Telephorus		1
Gods of the underworld		1
	Total:	*13*
Medical commands and prescriptions		
Asclepius		29
Zosimus		3
priest		3
doctor		2
mortals		5
unidentified		6
Aristides		1
	Total:	*49*
Other types of commands		
order to journey		9
order to write a speech		6
	Total:	*15*
Therapeutic bathing		21

The various dream-imagery appearing in Aristides' manifest dream content make evident that his dreams were dominated by persons and gods, all of whom were very close and important to Aristides in his waking life. In examining the manifest-content of these dreams, we may also notice a number of features that are also present in other dream accounts in ancient religious literature. Although there may exist stylistic parallels between the dreams in the *Sacred Tales* and other ancient dream texts, we are dealing with something more than mere literary motifs; in the case of Aristides we are most likely dealing an individual who recorded genuine dreams. E. R. Dodds correctly maintains that the dreams recorded the *Sacred Tales* are examples of culture-pattern dreams, that is, the structure of the dream is derived from materials culturally transmitted in the ancient world. Aristides' god-sent nocturnal visions are not simply the product of literary invention but rather actual psychological experiences informed by the categories of ancient religious knowledge.

ANCIENT GREEK DREAM LITERATURE AND THE SACRED TALES

The dream literature of ancient Greece contains distinct stylistic elements, which, as Dodds suggests, probably have a good deal of psychological significance. Many of these 'dream motifs' can also be found in the *Sacred Tales*.

Going back to pre-classical times, in Homer the dream frequently is treated as an objective entity. In the *Iliad* 2 the dream figure Nestor appears objectively in space in front of the passive dreamer, Agamemnon. In this passage Zeus sends a "Dream" to Agamemnon in order to tell him to prepare the Achaians for battle, since the gods of Olympus are now on their side. The dream takes on the form of Nestor and stands as an objective presence in front of the sleeping Agamemnon.[11] In the *Iliad* 22, 199–20, a different kind of dream is presented. Here there is a discussion of the psychological state of dreaming as opposed to a portrayal of dreaming as a kind of anthropomorphic phenomenon. A cogent insight drawn by Dodds from his study of the Homeric treatment of dream phenomena is that the language employed by later Greeks for describing their dreams is suggested by the Homeric vocabulary for describing dreams.[12] In Herodotus, the dream is not quite described as an objective entity yet dream figures appear to be objectively present in the dreams reported by Herodotus. For example, in the *Histories* II.141 the Ethiopian King Sabacos dreamt that a

---

[11] Cf. Iliad, 10., 496–497, 23.62–107; cf. William Stuart Messer, *The Dream in Homer and Greek Tragedy*, (New York, 1918), pp. 1–20. Also *Od.* 4.787–841; 6, 13–51.

[12] Dodds, *The Greeks and the Irrational*, op. cit., p. 105.

man stood by the side of his bed and advised him to gather together all of the Egyptian priests and cut them in half. Instead of following the advice of the dream-figure, Sabacos decided to leave Egypt and relinquish his control over that area. Further, in the *Histories*, V.56, Herodotus tells us about Hipparchus' dream occurring on the night before the great Panathenaic festival. Hipparchus was the ruler of Athens. In this dream, a tall and beautiful man appeared over Hipparchus' bed and spoke to him in riddles warning of his death. The next day, after he discussed the dream with dream interpreters, he forgot about the dream. Unfortunately, he participated in the procession during which he was assassinated.

Although such a portrayal of the dream as an objective entity is absent from the post-Homeric dream literature, vestiges of its influence can be felt in the language used by later Greeks to describe their dreams. Hence, the Greeks speak of seeing a dream (οναρ ιδειν) rather than having a dream. The phrase οναρ ιδειν hints at the externality of the dream vision. Modern society views dreaming as an internal psychological process yet the ancient Greeks spoke about the activity of dreaming in far more objective terms.

Similar to the dream accounts in Herodotus, the *Sacred Tales* never present the dream as an objective entity and yet in some passages Aristides describes the dream epiphany of a god just as Herodotus does, that is, in objective terms. For example, in S.T.I, 71 Asclepius appears to Aristides, who then grasped the god's head with his hands and begged him to save his ailing friend Zosimus. Aristides gives us the impression that Asclepius is physically present in the dream. Likewise, in S.T. IV, 57 it appears as if the dream figure of Plato actually enters the room and carries on a conversation with Aristides. In some dream-epiphanies, the deity stands before the reclining figure of Aristides as if the deity were physically present.[13]

There are certain features of Aristides' dreams which could be described as having passive qualities. For example, he states that he

---

[13] Cf. S.T. II.18, 41; in S.T.IV.60 the poet Sophocles stands in silence before the bedroom of Aristides.

sees a god or a person.¹⁴ Sometimes, he hears a voice.¹⁵ Dodds informs us that in the Greek tradition the dream is said to "visit" the dreamer (φοιταν επισκοπειν) as well as to "stand over" the dreamer (επιστηναι).¹⁶

As we have already noted, the god-sent dream is frequently attested to in ancient Greek literature. Artemidorus is quite familiar with three types of religiously significant dreams; first, there is the allegorical dream which requires interpretation; next, there is the prophetic dream which is a pre-enactment of a future event; lastly, there is the dream oracle which is characterized by the appearance of a deity or an equally impressive figure who reveals either what will occur or what perhaps should occur with respect to certain things.

A number of typical features are connected with this latter type of dream, and many of these dream epiphanies can of course be found in the *Sacred Tales*. Just as we noted that Aristides speaks of hearing a voice in his dream (φωνη δι ονειρατος), likewise Deubner reports that the hearing of a voice was a common element in the dream and visionary experiences of the ancients.¹⁷ In

---

¹⁴ The verb οραω is used in S.T.I.8, II.15, III. 4. Aristides states that he heard a voice in his dream in S.T.III.5, IV.39, IV. 86.

¹⁵ In the O.T., see Genesis, 20:3f; I Kings 3:4f, 9:2; in the Greek epic tradition see *Iliad* 2.23, 23.69, Od. 4.80f; cf. Oppenheim, op. cit., p. 188; for a discussion of this motif in Norse literature see G. D. Kelchner, *Dreams in Old Norse Literature and Their Affinities in English Folklore*, (Cambridge, England, 1935) pp. 87, 98, 107–8, 124. Here the sleeper upon awakening sees the 'person' of his dreams exiting the room.

¹⁶ Dodds, op. cit., pp. 105; 122N.16,17,18; φοιταν is used in this way in Sappho, *P. Oxy*, 1787; see also Herodotus 7.16, Plato, Phaedo 60E, etc.; references to the deity standing over the head of the dreamer are recorded in Herodotus, I.34.1; 2.139.1; 141.3, 5.56; in the Sumerian dream account of Eannatum "Stella of the Vultures" VI; 25–27, it is stated that "for him who lies (there)... he (the appearing deity) took his stand at his head." Cf. Oppenheim, op, cit., p. 189. See also Messer, *The Dream in Homer and Greek Tragedy*, op. cit., p. 6n, 22; p. 23, n. 68; p. 90, n. 248; cf. *Iliad* 24.683, Od 20.32. Since this motif appears in Greek and Near Eastern dream literature, one could say that there is a link between the two literary traditions.

¹⁷ L. Deubner, *De Incubatione*, (Leipzig, 1900), pp. 1–10.

De Genio Socratis 22 Plutarch relates the experience of Timarchos at the oracle of Trophonius who heard a voice of some unseen thing. Iamlichus tells us that one of the characteristics of *theopempoi*, or god-sent dreams, is that the dreamer sees a light and hears the voices of the gods.[18] φωσ ("light") appears to be a prominent feature in many epiphanies of the god.

As we have previously stated in Chapter Three, the author of Book XI of the *Metamorphoses* portrays Isis both in terms of the image of light and radiant beauty and similar sentiments are echoed in the writings of others such as Porphyry and Proclus.[19] Likewise, similar imagery involving light appears in the *Sacred Tales* when Aristides describes various "appearances" of Asclepius and other deities (cf. S.T.II.18, III.46).

In summary, Aristides is part of the "literary mainstream" when it comes to the reporting of dreams and visions in antiquity and therefore a careful analysis of his dream-visions can contribute to the ongoing task of developing a descriptive perspective of the nature of religious experience in Greco-Roman times. Aristides, as well as many others, were perhaps most receptive to this type of religious experience while in the state of semi-consciousness. Furthermore, many of the so-called typical features found in the dream accounts of Aristides and others are examples of "culture-pattern" dream phenomena and were actually present in the dream experiences themselves as opposed to being merely literary phenomena. On the one hand, it is likely that the ancient literary tradition of reporting dreams together with many of the typical features found in ancient dream-reports may have influenced the way in which Aristides interpreted and communicated his dream experiences to others. On the other hand, this same literary tradition of reporting dreams may have influenced the actual nature and contents of the dreams themselves, i.e., the culture-pattern dream.

---

[18] Jamblique, *Les Mysteres D'Egypte*, III.2, trans. Edouard Des Places (Paris, 1966), p. 100.

[19] Porphyry, *De Mysteriis*, II.8, II.2; S. Angus, *The Mystery Religions and Christianity*, (New York, 1925), p. 136 and Proclus, in *Plat. Remp.* I, cf. Angus, op. cit. p. 136.

CHAPTER SEVEN: A FUNCTIONAL ANALYSIS OF THE PERSONAL RELIGION OF AELIUS ARISTIDES

A PSYCHO-SOCIAL PERSPECTIVE

This chapter identifies some of the psychological elements involved in Aristides' entry into the cult of Asclepius, determining the psychological effects and functional value of Aristides' worship of Asclepius upon his personality. What were the positive and/or negative effects upon his personality in joining the cult of Asclepius? Aristides' religious behavior is not solely a by-product of psychological determinants nor is anxiety the primary source for understanding the nature of Aristides' piety, but psychological and social factors may have played a role in how Aristides' religiosity was expressed.

Although certain negative psychological elements may be found, the entirety of his religious life should not be equated with any of these psychic factors. In spite of his problems, his piety was a bright spot in his life. His religious experience represented a solution as opposed to a symptom of his difficulties.

It is difficult for the student of religion to offer any social-scientific explanation of the conditioning factors of an individual's religious attitude given the fact that there are so many interrelated variables that must be considered. When we seek to identify significant causal factors involved in the development of individual religious faith and experience it appears valid at the very least to distinguish between prominent social factors and important psychological experiences of the individual.[1]

Perhaps more than any other student of Freudian psychoanalysis, Erik Erikson was most responsible for correlating the psychological and social dimensions of human existence. In *Identity Youth and Crisis* Erikson delineates three processes which constitutes the nature of human existence; these three levels of human existence include the biological process consisting of the bodily organ processes, the social process consisting of individuals living together in groups and finally the ego process consisting of the individual attempting to develop a well-organized personality. Each process depends upon the other two so that if some impairment occurs in one of the three levels the other two usually experience some kind of consequence. Hence, the development of a pervasive sense of personal ego identity is reinforced by somatic, social as well as psychological forces. Erikson states,

> in discussing identity—we cannot separate personal growth and communal change, nor can we separate (as I tried to demonstrate in *Young Man Luther*), the identity crisis in individual life and contemporary crises in historical development because the two help to define each other. In fact the whole interplay between the psychological and the social, the developmental and historical, for

---

[1] A similar distinction is offered by Donald Capps in his excellent psychological study "Orestes Brownson: The Psychology of Religious Affiliation, *Journal For the Scientific Study of Religion*, vol. 7, (Fall, 1968), pp. 197–209. J. Milton Yinger develops a theory of religion in which individual tendencies and needs are seen as an important source of religion. Yinger's ideas have influenced our perspective on the religious experience of Aristides. Cf. J. Milton Yinger, *The Scientific Study of Religion*, (New York, 1970). Yinger states that religious experiences "are products, not only of the religious values and structures, but also of the full range of tendencies of the individuals involved and the social situations in which they find themselves. Therefore, we need a field perspective. Individuals are culturally prepared for certain experiences, both specifically religious values and by relevant secular norms," p. 143.

which identity formation is of prototypal significance could be conceptualized only as a psychosocial relativity.[2]

This dynamic relationship between the somatic, the psychological and the social realm is played out in Aristides' life. His physical illnesses play a vital role in the development of his religiosity as well as his personal identity which in turn mirrors a number of identifiable social upheavals occurring in the ancient Greco-Roman world. None of these factors justifies calling Aristides an "anxious soul" and yet such information sheds light on some of the interplaying factors affecting Aristides.

Aristides was a member of the upper class of Roman society. He lived in an era that Gibbon believed was one of the most peaceful and harmonious times in the entire history of civilization.[3] Even though the major urban centers of Asia Minor, including Aristides' home town Smyrna, as well as Pergamum and Ephesus had sustained a loss of their political and economic freedom due to the intervention of Roman rule, there is a good deal of evidence to suggest that the province of Asia Minor experienced a real prosperity under the Pax Romana.[4]

In respect to the second century CE, it is difficult to understand the clinging faith in the gods displayed in the lives of persons such as Aristides, given the optimistic socio-political circumstances of Roman society in this era. Not only was there political and economic well-being, but there was also a relative openness on the part of emperors, aristocrats and the poor alike to foreign religious beliefs and practices. The religious quest of Aristides was fairly characteristic of the new onslaught of religiosity occurring in his social world.[5] Peter Brown believes that the genesis of the "Age of Anxiety" occurs in the centuries following the conquests of Alexander

---

[2] Erik Erikson, *Identity, Youth and Crisis,* paperback ed., (New York, 1968), p. 23.

[3] B. P. Reardon, "The Anxious Pagan," Ontario Classical Association, (May 12th, 1973 Trent University), p. 82.

[4] Cf. David Magie, *Roman Rule in Asia Minor*, (Princeton, NJ, 1980), vol. 1, pp. 630–658.

[5] Peter Brown, "Approaches to the Religious Crisis of the Third Century A.D.," *English Historical Review*, vol. 83, (1972), p. 545.

the Great. It is probable that the immense social changes taking place in these times had ramifications upon subsequent developments in the realm of personal religion.

Although the Asia Minor provinces enjoyed the benevolent rule of the second-century Roman emperors, it is relevant to consider "the price at which the self-confidence of the Antonine and Severan periods had been bought."[6] The conquest of Asia Minor by the Hellenistic kings and Roman emperors resulted in the end of political freedom for aristocrats and peasants. Thus, Aristides and other aristocrats like him experienced a loss of liberty. The heightened concern in religious forms of healing as they are displayed in the cult of Asclepius may therefore be correlated to the destruction of political freedom.

A variety of social forces were responsible for bringing about the rise of late Hellenistic religious fervor and these social forces played a significant role in understanding Aristides' personal religious quest. These factors alone do not serve as an adequate explanation of the intense personal religious devotion that is described in the *Sacred Tales*, but if we refer back to Erikson's paradigm involving the three levels of human existence, it becomes very clear that somatic and psychological variables combined with social forces to produce significant causal factors in the development of Aristides' religious faith.

Aristides was living in a time when identity-formation presented problems since many of the traditional life-styles, societal values and social institutions of the classical era had either died out or were in the process of dramatic reformulation. The passing away of the old classical order of things created a cultural vacuum which subsequently was filled in part by new religious creeds, philosophies and dogmas. As a young adult, Aristides' personal identity was derived in a large measure from his close association with the cult of Asclepius. The sophist was twenty-four when he became a member of the healing cult. Thus, Aristides was groping to achieve psychic wholeness in an age that was struggling to find its ideologi-

---

[6] Peter Brown, op. cit. p. 545.

cal focus. Hence, we cannot separate Aristides' identity struggles from the profound changes occurring in his social world. [7]

For Aristides, it appears that he entered a period of psychological crisis prior to joining the cult of Asclepius. It is incorrect to refer to his adhesion to the cult as a case of "religious conversion." Religious conversion can be defined as a gradual or sudden process in which an individual moves away from a state of unhappiness or dividedness and moves into a state of wholeness and happiness.[8] Starbuck defines religious conversion as a kind of "unselfing."[9] The concept of conversion as most of us perceive it poses a conceptual problem when it is applied cross-culturally beyond the boundaries of the Western Judeo-Christian tradition. When we turn to the Greco-Roman tradition, the scholar Arthur Darby Nock has pointed out that we cannot locate "anything which can be called conversion."[10] According to Nock, the process of conversion involves a movement away from spiritual indifference or a past religious affiliation and a turning towards a new religious creed.

Whereas the Christian tradition contains many instances of this psychological transformation, most notably detailed in Augustine's *Confessions*, there is an absence of this point of view from the religious traditions of Greece and Rome. In pagan religious traditions, the primary emphasis is placed upon the reenactment of sacred myths by means of the performance of rituals as opposed to an emphasis upon individual adherence to a set of orthodox theological beliefs. In Christianity and Judaism, the new convert is required to renounce past sins and accept a new set of religious doctrines of the newly chosen religious institution. Nock points out that only the ancient philosophies insisted upon distinguishing between the higher kind of spiritual life and the lower profane existence. Of course, once Christianity became a dominant cultural force pagan individuals were inspired to return in penitence and enthusiasm to the faith of the past.[11]

---

[7] B. P. Reardon "The Anxious Pagan," op. cit., p. 82.
[8] William James, *The Varieties of Religious Experience*, op. cit, p. 157.
[9] E. D. Starbuck, *The Psychology of Religion*, (New York, 1903).
[10] A. D. Nock, *Conversion*, op. cit., p .14.
[11] Nock, *Conversion*, op. cit., p. 15.

Once Aristides became a member of the cult of Asclepius he did not look upon his past life with new eyes, nor did he seek to escape from the bondage to the flesh and the power of sin as in the case of Christianity. As noted in Chapter Three, unlike Augustine's *Confessions*, the *Sacred Tales* fails to provide us with a "history of the soul." Unlike Augustine, Aristides was not a "sick soul," and he does not review the events of his life from the standpoint of his new religious perspective. Unlike Marcus' *Meditations*, there is neither a sense of existential angst nor a pessimistic outlook on life. Unlike Christian writers such as St. Paul, there is an absence of moral reflection contained in the text. As Nock states, the pagans

> did not indeed desire to escape from sin, for it was in general assumed that moral evil, insofar as you were conscious of it, was something which of your own initiative you put from yourself before approaching the holy and not something from which you were delivered by approaching the holy.[12]

Unlike the typical Christian, Aristides was not set free from the power of evil demons, since the idea of the demonic is basically indigenous to Semitic culture. Although Asclepius saved Aristides from the control of Tyche in the present age through miraculous healings, the deity was not a giver of eternal life in the next age as in the Eleusianian mysteries, Christianity or Mithraism. Aristides' salvation was found in numerous miraculous healings performed either directly by Asclepius or through Aristides' performance of various "divine prescriptions." Just as the blessings of immortality were not conferred upon the devotee in the cult of Asclepius, the devotee was not expected to give up all of his past religious associations.

Religious exclusivism is primarily a phenomenon of the Judeo-Christian and Muslim traditions. Aristides' religious devotion did not have a single focus of attention. Even after his quasi-conversion experience, he continued to display affection toward Sarapis, Isis, Athena and others. Thus, when his beloved friend Zosimus died, Aristides called upon Sarapis for aid. The belief in

---

[12] Ibid.

the underworld—which is connected to the cult of Sarapis—most likely consoled him in his time of grief for Zosimus.[13] In the hymn *To Sarapis* Aristides discusses Sarapis' dominion over the heavens, earth and the underworld:

> He it is who assigns its place to each soul, according to the merit or demerit of its conversation upon earth, and the penal laws of the hereafter. By day He visits the regions above the earth; by night He executes the judgments upon which none living may look...[14]

Either Aristides failed to recognize or simply ignored the inherent contradictions concerning the hereafter in Egyptian and Greek religion respectively. Whereas Egyptian religion places a great stress upon the concept of the afterlife, Greek religion is mainly concerned with the present life. Eliade sums up the nature of religion in classical Greece by stating that in this tradition the individual is required to function with his own moral limitations, especially those that are assigned to him by his *moira*. Human wisdom results from the realization that human existence is finite and limited. The best path to take is to take advantage of the present moment. Thus, emphasis is placed upon youth, health, physical well-being, etc.[15]

Inasmuch as the cult of Asclepius recognized the importance of physical health and created an atmosphere for the promotion of healing, the cult may be viewed as an extension of the basic values and beliefs of Greek religion as they are outlined by Eliade. Moreover, the *Sacred Tales* should be understood in this context. Eliade notes that "since the gods had forced him not to go beyond his limits, man ended by realizing the perfection and, consequently the sacrality of the human condition."[16] Since the Greeks were interested in the sacralization of the human body, it is easy to see why they were also concerned with the scientific and religious forms of healing. Indeed, it is in ancient Greece where we see the early de-

---

[13] S.T.III.47.

[14] Edwyn Bevan, *Later Greek Religion*, (New York, 1927) p. 73.

[15] Mircea Eliade, *A History of Religious Ideas*, vol. 1, trans., Willard Trask, (Chicago, Ill., 1979), p. 262.

[16] Ibid., p. 282.

velopment of rational and non-rational healing techniques and in specific contexts such as the cult of Asclepius often both of these modes of healing exist side by side.

A good illustration of the protean character of the Hellenistic religious outlook is found in the short treatise *The Death of Peregrinus*, written by Lucian in the second century CE.[17] In this short sketch we are informed about the various religious exploits of Peregrinus; these exploits include a brief association with a Christian sect followed by a conversion to the philosophy of the Cynics. In 165 CE he decided to end his life at the Olympic Games by jumping into the flames of a funeral pyre.

Another example of pagan quasi-conversion is found in the life of Dio of Prusa.[18] This particular case concerns a conversion from rhetoric to philosophy. Since Aristides himself was a sophist, the example of Dio's movement away from rhetoric and a turning towards philosophy has special relevance. During the Flavian period, Dio was a rhetorician like Aristides and an enemy of the philosophical schools. During Domitian's reign, Dio was put in exile and during his exile he visited the Delphic oracle. He was told by the oracle to travel to the ends of the earth and so Dio became an ascetic wanderer. Dio presents a description of his philosophical pursuits in the treatise *De Exilio*. In this treatise Dio refers to himself as "the wanderer" and frequently compares himself to Odysseus who could be considered the "wanderer" *par excellence* in Greek literature.[19] Furthermore, he likens himself to other notable philosophers such as Socrates, Diogenes and Zeno. According to J. L. Moles, Dio appropriates these persons in order "to suggest that he is in the great tradition and to some extent can be mentioned in the same breath as the great Greeks of the past."[20]

---

[17] Lucian, "The Death of Peregrinus," in *Selected Satires of Lucian*, ed. and trans., Lionel Casson, (New York, 1962), pp. 364–381.

[18] Cf. Nock, *Conversion*, op .cit., p. 173f; also see J. L. Moles, "The Career and Conversion of Dio Chrysostom," *Journal of Hellenic Studies*, vol. 98, (1978), pp. 79–100.

[19] Cf., Moles, "The Career and Conversion of Dio Chrysostom," op. cit., p. 97.

[20] Ibid, p. 98.

In the *Sacred Tales*, Aristides employs a similar literary technique of comparing himself and his life to the life of Odysseus. Thus in the prologue of Book I he compares his story detailing the great feats of Asclepius to Helen's description of the deeds of Odysseus. There are several other references to Homer and the *Odyssey* in the *Sacred Tales*. For example, S.T.II.18 states that Asclepius quotes the *Odyssey* 19.547 when he addresses Aristides. Athena tells Aristides that the stories contained in the *Sacred Tales* are not idle tales but have important significance; she reminded him of the *Odyssey* and claims that he was Odysseus and Telemachus.[21] In S.T.II.60 Aristides likens the origins of his disease to the wondrous stories told by Odysseus to King Alcinous. One of his many sea voyages is described as a kind of odyssey in S.T. II.65. Like Dio, Aristides uses a similar literary convention of comparing himself to Odysseus as a way of casting himself and his plight in a heroic—and perhaps noble—light, yet he falls short of the narcissism that some have claimed.

THE PSYCHOLOGICAL VALUE OF ARISTIDES' ADHESION TO THE CULT OF ASCLEPIUS

When Aristides discusses his initial entry into the cult of Asclepius, he is really interested in talking about the origin of his illnesses rather than any type of spiritual transformation. Unlike Augustine, Aristides does not focus upon his entry into the religious life for apologetic purposes, nor does he portray himself as a "divided soul" or under the sway of sin prior to his association with the cult of Asclepius. Aristides' perspective on the events leading to his entry into the cult are only insignificant fragmentary events in the long history of his illnesses and have little importance except in forming the background to the beginnings of his physical maladies. Seen from the standpoint of the modern scholar, his illnesses created a "crisis" situation for the simple reason that the medical authorities at that time were unable to cure Aristides of his ailments. Hence, the crisis was to be resolved by turning to Asclepius for assistance. After Aristides gives his life over to the god, the god

---

[21] S.T.II.42.

assumes a supreme role in Aristides' life. He obeys the god's orders, even when the god's commands are extremely painful, since he does not wish to jeopardize his close relationship to Asclepius.

Festugiere has argued that before Aristides' crisis of faith, there was a period of common belief in which Aristides' faith in Asclepius was a lot like the faith of many typical believers. After Aristides sought out Asclepius in order to resolve the crisis brought on by his illnesses, the intensity of his religious faith dramatically increased. Although his illnesses continued to plague him after he had established his personal relationship with Asclepius, they provided him with the opportunity to receive from and give love to his savior god.[22]

The various prose hymns to the gods written by Aristides offer solid evidence that he paid heed to the traditional religious observances of his forefathers, even though the language of these hymns reveals that Aristides' faith in these gods was purely traditional in its nature. In the *Hymn to Zeus* it is Zeus who is the true deliverer. Asclepius, along with Apollo, Athena, Hera and Artemis are relegated into the background. Likewise, in the *Hymn to Sarapis* Asclepius is not even mentioned. All of this changes drastically after Aristides becomes seriously ill, although a resurgence of faith in Sarapis occurs after the death of Zosimus.

Seen from the perspective of modern psychology, Aristides' illnesses produced unusually strong feeling of helplessness. Since his doctors could not help him, his negative feelings grew wildly out of proportion so that there developed a need to believe in Asclepius as a means of obtaining a cure and hence bring about an end to his psychological crisis. The onset of Aristides' ailments occurred at a pivotal point in Aristides' life, namely, his emergence into adulthood and professional prominence. Their appearance at such a time in his life could be a response to the tremendous pressure he was experiencing at this time. In addition, just prior to leaving on his voyage to Egypt, shortly before his departure to Rome, Aristides' father suddenly died. The death of Eudamon no doubt added to the stress of the young man attempting a debut as a public speaker.

---

[22] Cf. Festugiere, *Personal Religion Among the Greeks,* op. cit., p. 99.

These factors alone do not explain the origins of Aristides' religiosity yet they shed light upon some of the conditioning factors involved. The prolonged history of Aristides' physical problems might be more easily accounted for if we could establish the specific deficiencies in his constitutional make-up or locate any residual psychobiological tensions derived from earlier stages of the lifecycle that could have been exerting their negative influences. Unfortunately such an investigation is limited due to the fact that Aristides is an historical figure who existed centuries ago and there is limited evidence available to us. However, we do have his dream diary and clues may be offered there.

The emotional pattern which occurs during the genesis of Aristides' physical illnesses and his first encounter with Asclepius repeats itself throughout the following seventeen years of his life. Henceforth, whenever he became ill, he experienced emotional insecurity concerning the outcome of the illness, which led to a re-strengthening of his connection to the god and his religious faith. It is likely that the renewal of religious faith brought about a corresponding renewal of his health. Furthermore, as a religious believer Aristides sought to uncover the god's wishes by means of interpreting his own dreams. Many of the divine prescriptions were painful, yet Aristides performed these actions since by their performance he was keeping his relationship to Asclepius alive.

THE PARADOXICAL DIVINE PRESCRIPTIONS

E. R. Dodds sees the performance of these irrational paradoxical and often violent divine prescriptions to be an expression of a deep-seated desire for self-punishment.[23] He is quite convinced that the unconscious manifests itself in Aristides' nocturnal visions in a decidedly negative and recalcitrant way. In general, Dodds sees little psychological value in such a religious system since the individual is "at the mercy of his own unconscious impulse, disguised as divine monitions…"[24]

---

[23] Dodds, *The Greeks and the Irrational*, op. cit., p. 116.
[24] Ibid.

Many of the rituals associated with the cult of Asclepius are religious rites and are not based upon any of the principles of modern medicine; these rituals can only be appreciated if they are viewed in their proper cultural context, namely, Greco-Roman religion and culture. However, from the standpoint of a modern person the performance of these "paradoxical prescriptions" seems puzzling; they do not appear to make much sense and have led some modern scholars to inquire into their psychological meaning.

If Dodds is correct in his assertion that Aristides is manifesting unconscious self-hatred by performing the paradoxical commands of Asclepius, it would be appropriate to identify the reasons for such masochistic tendencies. Unfortunately, Dodds nor any other commentator has provided us with any psychological explanation regarding the source of Aristides' frustration.

It is necessary to explore Aristides' psychic world further and seek to locate the crux of his problem. Aristides is not consciously aware of his desire for self-punishment. The majority of his religious rituals and acts are actually performed with a different intention which could be described in positive terms: they are intended to bring about the healing of his body. Thus, in S.T. III.13 it appears that in order to avert the imminent danger of a shipwreck Asclepius orders Aristides to overturn a skiff on the harbor. The contrivance of a shipwreck in the harbor symbolized the more dangerous threat of actual shipwreck at sea. By performing this ritual and triumphing over the lesser situation, Aristides was able to avoid the "real" danger. In this sense his behavior has positive overtones and yet most commentators have characterized his behavior mostly in negative terms.

REDUCTIONIST STUDIES OF THE PAST

Beginning in 1798 with the publication of an article "La Malittia Tredecennale D'Aelius Aristides" by the Italian physician Malacarne, the religious experience of Aristides has been the subject of intense scrutiny and negative criticism.[25] According to

---

[25] V. Malacarne, "La Malattia Tredecennale d'Aelius Aristides Sophista," *Scelti Sulle Scienze E Sulle Arti*, vol. 20, 1798, pp. 343–378.

Malacarne, Aristides is a hypochondriac who suffered from various physical ailments resulting from a mental aberration, e.g. hysteria. In addition to having rheumatism, Aristides had a personality problem consisting of a narcissistic urge to create vivid dreams about himself and the god Asclepius. Aristides' religious visions are explained away by supposing that the temple priests must have drugged their patients; the patients subsequently mistook the priests, who donned the clothes of Asclepius, for the god. Of course, Malacarne's ideas are not based on any solid evidence, but rather reveal an unconscious tendency to discredit pagan religiosity as it is manifested in the case of Aristides.

Moving forward to the twentieth century, we encounter continued negative characterizations of Aristides' character and religious behavior, most notably in the 1972 study of Aristides and his religiosity *Les Reves dans Discours Sacres d'Aelius Aristides*, by Gabriel Michenaud and Jean Dierkins.[26] These scholars employ the methods of Freudian psychoanalysis in order to analyze the sophist's dreams. These authors diagnosed Aristides in the following way: Aristides believed that he had a physically inferior body, even though he did not suffer from any acute physical illness, as is illustrated by his generally good vascular reactions upon taking his warm baths. Due to the fact that he was a hypochondriac, Aristides was unable to enjoy any physical satisfaction. Thus, the sophist turned to non-material pursuits such as rhetoric which freed him from any social responsibility. Out of his repression and detachment from the world developed an all-encompassing narcissistic tendency. As a result, Aristides derived more satisfaction from a supernatural entity than from his earthly companions. These scholars classify Aristides as a masochistic exhibitionist; he is also an example of the anal-retentive personality which is defined as an individual who orients himself towards the equilibrium of his various psycho-biological tendencies and functions.

During the anal stage of development, Freud noted that the infant learns to control the sphincters and by means of acquiring this power the child develops a new sense of freedom and inde-

---

[26] Gabrien Michenaud and Jean Dierkens, *Les Reves dans les "Discours Sacres" d'Aelius Aristide*, op. cit.

pendence from his parents. In some cases, the child becomes oriented towards the rigid control of his emotions and instinctual processes as opposed to the liberation of these psychic forces; an attitude of coldness and egocentrism develops. Other persons are disregarded unless they can be used for one's personal gain and interests.

Michenaud and Dierkens argue that Aristides' hostility towards others, his narcissism, his single-minded devotion to the god Asclepius, and his ever-present concern for his digestive problems all indicate that he displays many of the features of the anal-retentive personality. Furthermore, he is a hypochondriac of the first order: his symptoms are of the psychosomatic variety and are frequently encountered in hypochondria. He is totally preoccupied with himself and his health.

This psychological portrait of Aristides is far too harsh and leaves several unanswered questions. Michenaud and Dierkens' attempt to uncover the source of Aristides' psychic problem is rather superficial. Rather than seeing Aristides in the context of his society and relating his personal struggles to the cultural context in which they occur these scholars remove him from the historical circumstances in which he lived, and interpret his religiosity as a product of his neurosis. Hence, they fail to notice the numerous parallels between Aristides' religiosity and various religious trends of his era. These scholars fail to see the positive dimension of Aristides' piety. These scholars are correct in their assertion that Aristides is a troubled individual yet they are incorrect to reduce Aristides' religiosity to a product of his neurosis.

Even though psychoanalysis can be enlisted as an investigative tool to show that Aristides perhaps had a variety of neurotic tendencies, it does not follow that his religious behavior should therefore be classified purely as a pathological symptom and devoid of any positive spiritual significance. Undoubtedly, there is unconscious projective material in Aristides' religious experiences, as is indicated by his faithful performance of many painful divine prescriptions. Likewise, some the contents of his dreams reveal deep-seated psychological conflicts, yet these scholars fail to mention any positive value associated with Aristides' religious behavior. Instead, they seem content in simply pointing to the pathological implications.

TAKING THE RELATIVIST APPROACH

In spite of the shortcomings of the study conducted by Michenaud and Dierkens, it does raise interesting questions. When studying individuals from different cultures and/or different historical eras, what criteria can be used to determine whether or not a particular type of behavior such as the performance of painful divine prescriptions can be labeled "normal" or "abnormal"? To put it another way, what criteria are required for determining whether or not a particular pattern of behavior occurring in a particular spatio-temporal location is pathological? The answer is that the behavior must be judged relative to the culture in which it occurs.

The field of anthropology has provided us with a useful, well-developed and unbiased set of conceptual tools for answering this question. In her essay "Anthropology and the Abnormal," Ruth Benedict presents what might be termed the relativistic position regarding mental illness; Benedict claims that the categorical distinction between normality and abnormality is largely culturally determined.[27] Hence, what is judged to be abnormal in one cultural setting may be characterized in another cultural context as completely normal. In modern American society, the visionary and mystic are regarded in negative terms as aberrant types of individuals yet in other cultures they are valued as highly respected individuals. Benedict states "it is clear that culture may value and make socially available even highly unstable human types."[28]

Benedict's relativistic position should perhaps also be coupled with the realization that there are some universal biological criteria by which behavior is judged. In his article "Religious Systems as Culturally Constituted Defense Mechanisms," Melford Spiro defines some of these criteria.[29] First, any organic characteristic which, like cancer, produces death or leads to inefficient function-

---

[27] Ruth Benedict, "Anthropology and the Abnormal," in *Human Values and Abnormal Behavior*, ed. Walter D. Nunokawa, (Chicago, Ill., 1965), pp. 50–62.

[28] Ibid, pp. 52–53.

[29] Melford Spiro, "Religious Systems As Culturally Constituted Defense Mechanisms" in *Context and Meaning in Cultural Anthropology*, ed. Spiro, (New York, 1965), pp. 100–117.

ing is biologically abnormal. On this basis, Spiro claims that any condition which produces these effects including those characteristics of a particular organism and its behavior is pathological. Hence, if a religious belief or behavior is maladaptive or reduces the organism's ability to function efficiently, then viewed in biological terms, that belief or behavior is pathological or "abnormal." In respect to psychological and social processes, Spiro states that any resolution of tension in the individual which results in the impairment of psychological, social, or cultural functioning can be regarded as a universal indication of pathology.

If a religious belief prevents an individual from adapting to nature and society, then that belief can be labeled as "pathological" since the life of the individual is put in jeopardy. Spiro qualifies himself by stating,

> although the criteria by which behavior is judged may be universally applicable... the judgments based on these criteria are necessarily relative to the sociocultural context within which behavior occurs.[30]

Clearly, certain aspects of Aristides' piety—in particular the performance of certain irrational, painful "divine prescriptions" such as running outside unshod in the dead of winter—may appear to be biologically maladaptive since they do not appear to possess any positive health benefits. If positive health benefits were the result of their performance, then we would be hard-pressed to consider them in negative terms. Even though these paradoxical orders of the god were quite prevalent in the cult of Asclepius in Hellenistic times, as is illustrated by the Epidaurian inscriptions, nevertheless these activities must be labeled as "pathological" if they can be determined to be biologically maladaptive. The real question then is whether or not these behaviors yielded any positive health benefits.

If a certain religious behavior such as the performance of "paradoxical" divine prescriptions can be established as being primarily maladaptive, this does not mean that entirety of Aristides' piety is biologically maladaptive, only the behavior under question. Since Aristides most likely suffered from psychosomatic ailments

---

[30] Ibid., p. 105.

which are obviously due to a psychological disturbance, it leads us to assume that the entirety of his religious experience is a by-product of his neurosis and therefore "pathological." Such an all-or-nothing approach should be avoided incorrect.

Although a modern psychologist might identify Aristides as a neurotic, his peers may not have perceived him in the same light. Fortunately, in the *Commentary on Plato's Timaeus* preserved in an Arabic translation we have available to us a noteworthy comment about Aristides' condition made by the famous medical doctor Galen.[31] Galen is talking about the difference between physical ailments originating in the mind and organic illness and states,

> I have seen many people whose body was naturally strong and whose soul was weak, inert and useless... and as to them, whose souls are naturally strong and whose bodies are weak I have only seen a few of them. One of them was Aristides, one of the inhabitants of Mysia. And this one man belonged to the most prominent rank of orators. Thus it happened to him, since he was active in teaching and speaking throughout his life, that his whole body wasted away.[32]

Even though Galen had a well-developed conceptual understanding of mental illness for the age in which he lived, he failed to detect Aristides' psychosomatic condition. Instead, Aristides is a consumptive. What impressed Galen the most about Aristides was the fact that while his body deteriorated, he was an active orator. Galen's comment represents the only extant opinion by a medical doctor who knew Aristides and was familiar with his physical condition.

It is a fact that in spite of his psychosomatic ailments, Aristides functioned as an active and respected member of his society, with the possible exception of the first two years of his illness

---

[31] Cf. ed. H. O. Schroder, "Galenus' In Platonis Timaeum comment fragmenta," 87, e 5–88, b5 in *Corpus, Medicorum Graecorum*, Supp. 1, (1934), p. 33. For Behr's translation, see *Aelius Aristides and the Sacred Tales*, op. cit., p. 105.

[32] Cf. Behr, op. cit., p. 105.

when he gave up his professional career as a sophist and lived in or near the temple. During this two-year period at Pergamum, Aristides vigorously pursued his dream quest; in some measure it resulted in a transformation in his personal identity since he emerged from this period with a renewed sense of direction and energy for pursuing the life of the sophist. Undoubtedly, his dream visions during this period played a significant role in the development of his psychological integration and fostered his sense of "special election."

An important evaluative question remains concerning Aristides' religious experience. In a scholarly work dealing with the early history of psychiatry *Madness in Society*, George Rosen has noted the positive psychological consequences of Aristides' adhesion to the cult of Asclepius.[33] Rather than viewing Aristides as a kind of marginal figure of the history of Graeco-Roman religion, Rosen employs Spiro's concept of religion as a culturally constituted defense mechanism in order to show that the cult of Asclepius, with its elaborate incubation practices, healing rituals, and dream-experiences all served an important integrative function in Aristides' psyche and provided him with a culturally sanctioned means for promoting psychic balance and the lessening of stress and anxiety. Rosen believes that for persons such as Aristides who exhibited psychological problems, it is within reason to assume that they could exist in their society in an adequate fashion "as long as the behavioral environment which they constructed for themselves did not result in undue psychological distortion and socio-cultural impairment."[34] Rather than falling into a state of withdrawal and complete maladjustment, Aristides appropriated the religious therapy of the cult of Asclepius for working out his problems and successfully warding off serious mental illness.

The value of Rosen's ideas resides in the fact that that this scholar's psychological assessment of Aristides' condition is based

---

[33] George Rosen, *Madness in Society*, (Chicago, Ill., 1968), p. 110f; cf. Spiro, M. "Religious Systems as Culturally Constituted Defense Mechanisms," in *Context and Meaning in Cultural Anthropology*, op. cit., pp. 100–117.

[34] Rosen, op. cit., p. 109.

primarily upon an understanding of the psycho-cultural norms of Aristides' society rather than chiefly upon the norms of modern rationality. Aristides' attention to his dreams, his devotion to Asclepius and his submission to the therapeutic rituals and medical procedures of the cult of Asclepius all can be understood as a positive attempt to achieve psychic integration through the mastery of unconscious anxiety. The painful irrational divine prescriptions represent an exception to the rule since in certain instances their performance could be construed as "biologically maladaptive." Furthermore, there appears to be a negative cycle involved with his physical maladies; Aristides was never able to completely rid himself of them because without them there would be no impetus to keep his religious relationship with Asclepius alive. In spite of this, Aristides was able to function more or less successfully in his society as a sophist of some repute largely because of the religious therapy provided by the cult of Asclepius.

CHAPTER EIGHT: AN ANALYSIS OF THE LATENT CONTENTS OF ARISTIDES' DREAMS

THE CROSS-CULTURAL APPLICATION OF PSYCHOANALYSIS

This chapter investigates the latent, hidden meaning of several of Aristides' dreams, enlisting the tools of modern psychology and psychoanalysis to uncover the meaning of the disguised symbolism contained in Aristides' dreams. We are not attempting to discredit Aristides' religiosity. By employing the tools of Freudian dream interpretation for exploring the dreams and conflicts of an historical figure such as Aristides, we are making certain assumptions regarding the universal applicability of Freudian concepts. Students of ancient society have been generally skeptical about the value of employing such methods.[1] Their main concern has to do with the universal applicability of Freudian theory to the study of history and culture. Ahistorical concepts such as the Oedipus complex, the Id and the Superego have never been shown to have universal relevance. Recently, Brooke Holmes interpreted the *Sacred Tales* as a literary work and dismissed the "outdated" technique of Freudian psychoanalysis for understanding Aristides' dreams.[2] The universal cross-cultural applicability of Freudian theory may appear ques-

---

[1] See "The Future of Dreams: From Freud to Artemidorus" in *Studies in Ancient Greek and Roman Society*, (Cambridge, 2004) ed., Robin Osborne, pp. 226–260.

[2] "Aelius Aristides' Illegible Body" in William V. Harris and Brooke Holmes, ed, *Aelius Aristides: Between Greece, Rome and the Gods*, (Leiden and Boston, 2008), p. 81.

tionable. On the other hand, it may seem unreasonable to contend that none of Freud's ideas have any relevance to historical research. It is our contention that an interdisciplinary methodology combining the tools of history and psychology has limited validity for studying a figure such as Aristides. The value of using Freudian psychoanalysis and other tools of the modern social sciences can only be determined by means of actually performing the task of interpretation. We will demonstrate that modern social scientific concepts including those developed by Freud can provide a meaningful interpretive framework for understanding the dream material presented in the *Sacred Tales*. As Thomas W. Africa notes,

> despite impressive neo-Freudian contributions to modern history, ancient historians are cautious about the utility of psychohistory for Greek or Roman studies where sources are shaky or inadequate... The proof of a hypothesis lies in demonstration.[3]

The credibility of our interpretation should be based upon its internal consistency and its ability to clarify the psychological factors influencing the nature of Aristides' religiosity.

One might hesitate to use the principles of Freudian psychoanalysis for the interpretation of the dreams of Aristides simply because the universality of Freudian dream symbolism has never been proven. On the contrary, most studies on this subject have tended to support the opposite notion, namely, that Freudian interpretative concepts are for the most part culture-bound, reflecting Judeo-Christian social values and have limited value when applied outside the horizon of the Western world. In fact, most, if not all, of Freud's theoretical concepts may not apply whatsoever to the study of ancient culture.

If one examines these issues a little closer however, one can discern that there are grounds for supposing at least in theory that many of Freud's central ideas have cross-cultural applicability for interpreting the dreams of persons from other cultures and times.

---

[3] Thomas Africa, "Mask of the Assassin: A Psychohistorical Study of M. Junius Brutus" *Journal of Interdisciplinary History*, vol. VII, n. 4, (Spring, 1978), pp. 558–612.

If this is true, then they would certainly have applicability for interpreting the meaning of Aristides' dreams. Lincoln and Seligman, both students of Freud, point out in their cross-cultural study of dreams that many of the so-called latent desires and wishes of the individual find themselves expressed in dreams containing certain types of stereotypical imagery and symbols, with the meaning of the imagery remaining somewhat constant in a variety of cultural contexts. In this regard Lincoln and Seligman state,

> the same forms and symbols, however, do not arise not only in the dreams of persons undergoing analysis, but in dreams independently reported from all quarters of the world. Although the meanings may vary for different individuals, the same meanings for particular symbols and forms appear repeatedly in all parts.[4]

The ideas that tend to be expressed repeatedly throughout all cultures and times pertain to the physical body, the individual's relationship with the family, birth, sexuality, love and death. Numerous dreams recorded in the *Sacred Tales* make reference to the condition of Aristides' physical body. Dreams involving water in the *Sacred Tales* may have reference to intrauterine life and the trauma of birth. Furthermore, there are various images appearing in Aristides' dreams which have sexual significance. Of course, the manifest-content of dreams differ from one culture to another yet the latent significance of the dream symbols may have reference to similar psychological forms appearing in different cultural groups.

In discussing man's various drives, such as the drive for power, the desire for pleasure, and the drive for approval from one's parents, one must remember that all of these needs including hunger and sex "are not fixed as to form of expression and fulfillment—man's nature his passions and anxieties, his thoughts and acts are a cultural product."[5] Whereas Freud claimed that the Oedipus complex is a universal biological phenomenon, modern an-

---

[4] J. S. Lincoln and C. G. Seligman, *The Dream in Primitive Culture*, (Baltimore, 1935), p. 17.

[5] Thompson, *Psychoanalysis: Evolution and Development. A Review of Theory and Therapy*, (New York, 1950), p. 144.

thropological research has shown that it is not universal but rather occurs primarily in specific cultural settings, namely in monogamous patriarchal social orders.[6] For example, Bronislaw Malinowski showed that the Trobrian islanders, a Melanesian matriarchal tribe of primitive peoples were free from any of the aggressive feelings against the father that are usually associated with the Oedipus complex.[7] Even though one would hesitate to claim the universal validity to Freud's theories, many Freudian concepts have interpretative appeal in the case of Aristides' dreams.

THE PSYCHOANALYTIC INTERPRETATION OF ARISTIDES' RELIGIOSITY AND DREAMS

It is difficult, if not impossible, to isolate Aristides' psychic problems with absolute certainty by means of employing any particular interpretative method including Freudian theory; our goal is therefore to develop a theoretical model that makes sense out of disparate pieces of the puzzle of Aristides' waking and unconscious dream life. Our starting-point is to seek the connection between the manifest-contents of Aristides' dreams originating from his waking experience at the pre-conscious level of the mind and the latent contents existing at the unconscious level. For example, the manifest-content of many of Aristides' dreams involve his parents and other significant others such as the god Asclepius and his friend Zosimus. These manifest contents of his dreams may serve as a kind of thread that leads us to related psychological issues existing on the unconscious level. A cursory glance at the manifest contents of Aristides' dreams shows that he derived an exaggerated amount of emotional gratification from his religious bond with Asclepius. It is tempting to consider the possibility that there was a time in his past when this need went unfulfilled. Perhaps in Aristides' childhood he suffered from a loss of instinctual satisfaction due to a disruption of his object-attachment to his parents.

---

[6] See *Man and His Culture: Psychoanalytic Anthropology After 'Totem and Taboo'*, ed. Warner Muensterberger, (London, 1969), p. 87.

[7] See B. Malinowski, *Sex and Repression in Savage Society*, (New York, 1927).

His psychological needs may then have found their gratification as an adult by means of his close relationship to the god Asclepius. From a Freudian perspective, this gratification via Asclepius involves the unconscious utilization of a defense mechanism called "sublimation" whereby an individual obtains pleasure through a non-sexual means, and in this case, by means of a religious relationship to the god Asclepius. From a psychoanalytic perspective, Aristides' religiosity represents a sublimated version of the struggle for instinctual pleasure occurring in the earliest years of childhood. In the Freudian scheme of things, his illnesses as an adult could be seen as a symbolic manifestation or recapitulation of the traumatic situation of object-loss in childhood. The psychosomatic ailments then function as an opportunity for Aristides to gain mastery of his fears and anxieties existing at the unconscious level.

Nowhere in the *Sacred Tales* is there any indication that Aristides had any strong romantic ties with anyone of the opposite sex. This does not necessarily mean that he did not have any romantic inclinations towards women. However, it is interesting that females are rarely mentioned at all the *Sacred Tales* and seldom appear in his dreams. We already know that Aristides devoted a great deal of energy to his work as a sophist and his relationship to his god yet there are few details about his relations to other friends and associates. We know that Zosimus, Aristides' family retainer, was his closest friend. Aristides' deep attachment to Zosimus is clearly demonstrated when Zosimus dies. Aristides grieved a good deal over Zosimus' death and it is at this time that Aristides turned his attention to the cult of Sarapis, which, unlike the cult the cult of Asclepius, had associated with it a strong belief in the doctrine of the afterlife. Immediately following Zosimus' death, Aristides found solace in his worship of the Egyptian gods of the dead.[8]

Given such strong ties to Zosimus, one can only speculate about whether or not Aristides had homosexual feelings towards Zosimus. The pair often travelled together, as is described in S.T.I.69f where Aristides implores Asclepius to save Zosimus from imminent danger. In S.T.I.23 we are presented with a blatant homosexual dream. Here Aristides, accompanied by his teacher Alex-

---

[8] S.T.II.47

ander, approaches the emperor. After Alexander salutes the emperor and Aristides follows suit, the emperor requests him to step forward and kiss him. Aristides replies that he cannot since he is a worshipper of Asclepius. Other homosexual references can be found in a few bathing dreams although nothing very overt is mentioned.[9] In general, Aristides was surrounded in his waking life by males and this fact is repeated for the most part in his dream life. There is no evidence of overt homosexuality in his waking life.

Undoubtedly a large amount of psychic energy was channeled by Aristides into his work as a sophist, yet this activity was also "religious" in the sense that Aristides considered himself to be a divinely-inspired writer and speaker. Certainly, the primary means by which Aristides received psychological support and attained a sense of well-being in the universe was through his participation in the rituals and religious activities of the cult of Asclepius; it is through his close association with this religious group that he developed a sense of trust enabling him to conquer the most negative feelings of anxiety, depression and withdrawal that are usually connected with psychosomatic illness.

As previously discussed, it is likely that Aristides experienced a significant disruption of some sort of the bond uniting him as an infant with either one or both of his parents. All of the evidence presented in the *Sacred Tales* suggests that Aristides was not raised by his parents. Zosimus and other servants of his family were given the task of raising the boy. Thus, we read in S.T.IV.54 that Epagathus, one of Aristides' foster fathers, was responsible for first raising the boy. It was Epagathus who first introduced Aristides to the art of divination.

Upper class Roman child-rearing practices during the Empire period tended to alienate the child from its mother. Tacitus informs us of the changed habits of the aristocracy in the upbringing of children:

> In the old days, each Roman child born in wedlock was not brought up in the back-bedroom of some slave girl nurse, but in its mother's bosom... Now the new-born

---

[9] Cf. S.T.I.21, I. 34

infant is handed over to some little Greek serving-maid who has the help of some other slave chosen from the rest of the household, usually the most worthless and totally unfitted for an important task.[10]

The solemn emperor Marcus Aurelius was entrusted to the care of nurses after his birth.[11] His mother, Lucilla, probably had little to do with her son for a while. Such child-rearing practices which routinely included a separation of the infant from his parents perhaps produced difficulties for children trying to develop a sense of "basic trust," to use Erikson's terminology, during the first stage of the life cycle. In Aristides' later life, religious themes would again manifest the unresolved portions of this infantile psychosocial crisis. It is during the period when Aristides first fell ill and developed his attachment to Asclepius that we see the emergence of infantile patterns of experience in his quest for identity. These recapitulated infantile patterns of experience find their definition and organize themselves around Aristides' pervasive sense of abandonment by his parents and his overwhelming need to reestablish once again their parental authority in his life.

Unfortunately, we do not have any direct reference made by Aristides to any early childhood trauma involving a severing of the bonds of affection and trust between himself and his parents. If such an event took place, it would be mostly covered up by the powerful repressive forces of the unconscious and so we are reduced to making inferences based upon an examination of his dreams, his waking behavior and psychosomatic illnesses. The situation is further complicated by the fact that when dealing with the subject of psychic trauma, it is necessary to distinguish between fact and fantasy. Any attempt to determine whether or not Aristides was abandoned by his parents must include consideration of whether or not Aristides perceived himself in those terms, regardless of what actually happened in objective terms.

In the *Sacred Tales*, Aristides displays a good deal of affection for his family retainers, especially Zosimus, while he displays a

---

[10] Tacitus, *Dial.*, pp. 28–29.
[11] Cf. V. *Marci* 2.1.

complete indifference to his parents. Given the fact that his diary is written with a religious purpose in mind and is not a "history of the soul," there is little reason for him to mention his childhood, his parents and growing up. He does take the time to frequently mention Zosimus and his other family servants in the context of discussing life at the temple and so forth. However, since Zosimus, Epagathus and others were given the duty of raising Aristides, it should not come as a surprise if he transferred some of his frustrated feelings of affection for his parents to these individuals. To use Freudian terminology, Zosimus and Epagathus functioned as parental substitutes for Aristides.

Studies on the nature of separation anxiety have shown that after the initial separation from the mother the child has the experience of becoming transiently attached to a series of mother-substitutes.[12] Investigators have discovered that femininity is not a prerequisite for playing the role of the mother-substitute. In order to function successfully as a mother-substitute the individual must be a person that is very familiar and well acquainted with the child. If it is correct that Aristides was separated from his parents and that he interpreted his separation from them in traumatic terms, then it would follow that there would be a need for some sort of parental-substitute, a role which was fulfilled by Zosimus, upon whom Aristides greatly depended for emotional support for many years. Zosimus appears in several of Aristides' dreams. For example, in S.T.III.3 Aristides dreams that he is being carried alone on a raft in the middle of the Mediterranean Sea off the coast of Egypt. As his raft drifts towards land, Aristides begins to experience a noticeable feeling of distress; suddenly the figure of Zosimus appears on dry land with a horse. Somehow Aristides is able to land his raft on the shore and accept the horse.

From the Freudian perspective, the dream-image of being alone on a raft in the middle of the sea could be interpreted symbolically as the withdrawal and isolation experienced by the ego when it is forced in early childhood to separate itself of its libidinal attachment to the mother. The raft symbolizes the ego riding on

---

[12] See especially John Bowlby, "Separation Anxiety," *The International Journal of Psychoanalysis*, vol. XLI, pts 2–3, pp. 89–113, (1960).

the sea of the unconscious; since Aristides' libidinal needs are no longer attached to their original object, this produces a feeling of distress which is expressed in the dream. The appearance of Zosimus and the horse represents the transference of psychic energy formerly directed towards Aristides' parents which is now directed to Zosimus. Frequently, the appearance of animals in dreams symbolizes the instincts.[13] Thus, the horse in this dream further underscores the re-emergence of the instincts. In Aristides' adulthood, Zosimus functioned more or less as a friend than a guardian.

In a few of Aristides' dreams there is manifested a good deal of anxiety.[14] We have already noted that the psychological authenticity of Aristides' dream diary is supported by the presence in it of these anxiety dreams, including those appearing in S.T. I.9I.13 and I.22. The appearance of anxiety in these dreams could be seen as an attempt by Aristides' psyche to review certain anxiety-producing situations in his life with the purpose of finally coming to terms with certain unresolved issues. In the post-traumatic anxiety dream, there is usually a confrontation with the overwhelming negative stimulus appearing either directly or in symbolic form.

In each of the previously noted anxiety-dreams there appears the image of some pointed object that is threatening to injure Aristides. Whereas in S.T.I.9 it is a finger, it is a horn of a bull in S.T. I.13. In S.T. I.22 Aristides is threatened by a knife while in S.T. I.28 Aristides dreams that he is choking on a sharp bone caught in his throat. A Freudian interpretation of these dream images would suggest that we are dealing with phallic imagery and their appearance indicates the existence of unconscious sexual conflicts.

In S.T. I.21f we read that Aristides dreamt that he was in a warm bath. Suddenly some men armed with daggers appear accompanied by other suspicious characters. These men approach Aristides and tell him that they were accused of some unknown thing by other men. After he is surrounded by these men, Aristides

---

[13] Emil A. Gutheil, *The Handbook of Dream Analysis*, 2nd, ed., (New York, 1966), p. 136.

[14] Dodds has an excellent discussion of Aristides' anxiety dreams to which I am indebted. Cf. *Pagan and Christian in An Age of Anxiety* and, op. cit., p. 41f.

becomes anxious yet he does not want to show his feelings. Suddenly, he is travelling along some path where he encounters an enormous vault. Again he experiences fear because he thinks these men might attack him inside the vault. To his relief, he passes through the vault and emerges into his hometown of Smyrna.

From a Freudian perspective, the men equipped with daggers appear as an expression of unconscious hostility and perhaps fear of castration. On the one hand, they seem to be personifications of hostility and perhaps Aristides' unconscious fear of castration by his father. At the same time, these figures confide in Aristides, telling him that they have been accused of some unidentified thing. Hence, his feelings towards them are slightly ambivalent just as Aristides' feelings towards his aloof and distant father must have been ambivalent. These men force Aristides to leave the security of his bath, just as the fear of reprisal and even castration ultimately causes the child to give up the desire for union with the ultimate security, i.e., the mother. We must remember that castration-anxiety is a product of fantasy, yet as Freud has shown time and time again, fantasy sometimes has a far greater effect on the psyche than reality.

The fear of castration is present in another dream prescription. In a dream Aristides is commanded by Asclepius to cut off one of his fingers. Castration anxiety as it appears in Aristides' dreams can easily be related to the Oedipus Complex which implies that such a psychological phenomenon was not unknown in ancient Greek culture. If one turns to the works of Artemidorus, we find that he understood the complexities of interpreting dreams in which an individual has sexual intercourse with his mother. Artemidorus writes, "the case of one's mother is both complex and manifold and admits of many different interpretations—a thing not all dream interpreters have realized." Artemidorus continues by stating that,

> the fact is that the mere act of intercourse by itself is not enough to show what is portended… if anyone possesses his mother through face-to-face intercourse which some

would call the 'natural' method... it means that he and his father will become enemies because of... jealousy.[15]

Of course Artemidorus was not fully aware of the psychic significance of the Oedipal dream and was interested in analyzing it from the standpoint of his pseudo-scientific categories of dream interpretation. Nevertheless, his testimony supplies us with evidence that Oedipal conflicts were present in the dreams of the ancients. Some of these infantile fears are still being worked through in Aristides' unconscious, as his dream of the loss of a finger indicates.

Aristides displays anxiety sometimes while he is awake. For example, he tells us in S.T. I.7 that upon emerging from a bath he felt somewhat uncomfortable and his breathing became constricted. He interpreted this to be a sign that he should stop taking nourishment. Obviously, he believed that the bath was a place of security and he often experienced union with the god while he bathed. In the bath described above, upon its conclusion he once again experienced feelings of anxiety. It is possible that Aristides associated unconsciously the security of his ritual bathing with the security of his early childhood bond with his mother. Just as the disruption of the bath resulted in anxiety, likewise the severing of the ties to his mother produced massive anxiety.

Most likely, Aristides' illnesses performed the psychological function of permitting the ego to work out unconscious anxiety associated with certain early childhood events related to separation from his parents. Asclepius functions psychologically as an authority figure; it is the god who re-institutes parental authority and serves as the object of Aristides' affection. Although Aristides' experience of the divine is expressed through the imagery of the unconscious, this does not deny the validity of his religious experience, nor does it negate the idea of an objective realm of the spirit known by Aristides and other religiously-inclined individuals throughout human history. However, our psychological contentions about Aristides represent an illustration of an important point: a human being's experience of the holy is conditioned by

---

[15] Artemidorus, *Oneirocritica*, I.79; trans. Robert J. White, op. cit., p. 61.

unconscious forces. It is through his worship and devotion to Asclepius that Aristides strives to return to the time before the infant experiences all of the dualities and loneliness produced by the development of ego-consciousness.

Several commentators of the *Sacred Tales* have noted a deep narcissistic tendency on the part of Aristides that is frequently reflected in his concern with his illnesses and in his dreams. For example, he often compares his symptoms with his friends and he is convinced that no one suffers as greatly as he. In S.T.I.46–49 he tells us that the Emperor Marcus Aurelius and Lucius Verus paid him much attention. Throughout the text he repeatedly informs the reader about many of his rhetorical feats and the complements bestowed upon him by the god Asclepius. In one instance, Aristides describes an occasion when two household servants die during one of his illnesses and he tells us that the life of each servant was given up in exchange for his life.

Aristides' narcissistic behavior can be understood as a consequence of separation not accepted, or to use Freud's terminology, as the result of an overstimulation of consciousness due to object loss:

> When it happens that a person has to give up a sexual object, there quite often ensues a modification in his ego which can only be described as a reinstatement of the object within the ego...[16]

When the parental object is lost, the love that went out to it is partially redirected to the ego.

> Since the loss of the beloved object is not accepted, the human ego is able to redirect the human libido to itself only to be deluding the libido by representing itself as identical with the lost object.[17]

Aristides' vain outlook on life may have been fostered by means of transferring affection from the parental object to himself. The

---

[16] Sigmund Freud, *Collected Papers,* ed. J. Riviere, (New York, 1924–50), p. 458.

[17] Ibid.

transformation of object-libido implies an abandonment of sexual aims, a process of de-sexualization, which characterizes his self-concept as well as his relationship to Asclepius. From a Freudian point of view, his egotism and his gods are in many ways shadowy substitutes for the original sexual object. However, his narcissism is balanced by the religious function of his psyche. Asclepius combats the "inflation of the ego" since Aristides is aware that he alone cannot magically cure himself. The faculty of healing is given to Asclepius and it is not through any magical actions of his own that Aristides is healed of his various physical ailments. Besides Asclepius, there are a number of other symbols of authority that appear in Aristides' dreams. For example, in S.T. I.36 another narcissistic dream is recorded. In the dream Aristides is accompanied by two rulers, Antoninus and a younger unnamed emperor. Aristides is led by them on a walk around a drainage ditch surrounding the city. Aristides walks along in the middle between the two of them. Each time he tried to move to one side the younger emperor was able to do this before he could. As a result, Aristides remained in the same place, in the middle between two emperors.

On several occasions, Freud interpreted the appearance of animals in dreams to be a symbolic expression of the instincts. Animals appear in Aristides' dreams in several instances. In one of Aristides' more vivid dreams, he is walking inside the temple of Asclepius. While he was walking and talking to some temple priests, one of his slippers fell off from one of his feet. A priest picked it up and gave it to him. As he was bending over to receive it, a bull suddenly came up to him, causing him to be afraid. To his surprise, the bull did not hurt him, but rather pressed up against his right knee. Apparently upon waking from his dream, Aristides noticed a small sore beneath his right knee which eventually proved to be good for his upper digestive tract.[18]

From a psychoanalytic perspective, the bull could be interpreted as a symbol of the instincts. In the dream the bull appears when Aristides is completely off-guard and yet instead of attacking, the bull merely presses against him in a soothing way. Hence, this dream could be interpreted as a message from the Aristides' un-

---

[18] S.T.I.12–13.

conscious telling him not to be afraid of the forces of the unconscious which may seem terrifying to Aristides but actually possess a healing, creative function.

As previously discussed, Asclepius is the object of numerous psychic projections involving a transferring of libidinal energy that was previously attached to Aristides' parents that is now channeled to the healer god. From a psychological perspective, the god is a projection of some of Aristides' deepest unconscious wishes. Hence, it is interesting to note that in a dream recorded in S.T.I.17–18 the following dream imagery appears. While Aristides is in Smyrna, he goes to the temple in the evening accompanied by his friend Zeno. While the pair offer prayers to the god, Aristides' eyes fall upon a statue of himself which right before his eyes turns into a statue of Asclepius.

Rather than interpreting this dream as another example of Aristides' narcissism, as other commentators have done, it is probably an attempt by Aristides' unconscious to tell him that there is an intimate bond uniting him to his god. The dream image is trying to indicate to him that it is he who is the source of all of the positive virtues bestowed upon him by his god and his god is in many respects a reflection of the potentialities of his hidden self. A similar dream is recorded in S.T. IV.50f dealing with Asclepius' remark that Aristides is "The One," meaning the god. Likewise, "Theodorus" is the name given to Aristides by Asclepius. This name means "God given."

The last dream recorded in the *Sacred Tales* is highly illustrative of several of the key elements in Aristides' psychic life and we conclude our psychological analysis of Aristides with a discussion of this dream. In the dream Aristides is walking in the direction of the Lyceum and observes a temple in the distance which he decides to enter. As he climbs the temple steps some men appear who are standing around the outside of the temple walls. These men are described by Aristides as seeming like those who hold out olive boughs for sale in the market. Aristides continues ascending the steps of the temple and when he reaches the doors of the temple a little boy appears and offers to sell him three eggs. Suddenly Aristides experiences an uneasy feeling because he feels that he should have bought the eggs from the boy instead of refusing to purchase them. Therefore, he turns around and takes the eggs. He then went up the stairs and when he reached the top he gave the eggs to a man in charge of the sacred precinct standing by a pillar. This man desired to add one more egg to the other three.

The main religious image present in this dream is "an ascent." Aristides is ascending the steps leading upwards to the temple doors. The historian of religion, Mircea Eliade, suggests that the image of the staircase and the ladder are pre-eminently symbols of the passage from the profane mode of being to the sacred mode of being. In archaic religion, the ascent of a stairway is regarded as a rite of passage, whereas in Freudian thought, the ascent of a stairway in a dream is described as a disguised expression of sexual desire. According to Eliade, Freud's interpretation is one-sided even though Eliade admits that the sexual significance of the ascent of the stairway, which was discovered by Freud, implies a kind of rite of passage. Eliade states,

> to infer that the patient who is ascending the staircase in a dream is thereby gratifying a sexual desire buried in the unconscious—this is still a way of saying that in the depths of his being, the patient is struggling to get out of a situation in which he is stuck, a negative sterile situation.[19]

The Freudian interpretation of the image of the staircase does not directly contradict the religious understanding of the image as it appears in myth and ritual. In this sense, Aristides' ascent of the temple steps symbolizes a transcendence which can be understood either in a religious or sexual framework of meaning. As Eliade points out, religious transcendence has sexual connotations just as human sexuality has religious overtones. Aristides' religious experiences have religious as well as sexual implications. Likewise, his ascent of the steps to the temple in his dream has a two-fold meaning.

As an adult it is through his desexualized religious relationship that Aristides is able to come to terms with some of his uncon-

---

[19] Mircea Eliade, *Myths, Dreams and Mysteries*, (New York, 1967), p. 117. For a discussion of the four psychic functions of the human mind, see *Man and His Symbols*, ed. C. G. Jung, (Garden City, New York, 1964), p. 61.

scious problems associated with the disruption of the bonds uniting himself with his parents and especially his mother. Asclepius functions psychologically as the provider of security and protection that Aristides once had and lost as a child. In this particular dream, the sexual significance of Aristides' religious life is underscored by the presence of sexual symbolism, namely, the men standing by the temple holding something like olive boughs.

Psychoanalysis has shown that the unconscious speaks to us through the language of dream symbolism. In this particular dream the unconscious is attempting to speak through the symbols of the ascent and the image of the "egg." We have discussed the significance of the ascent. What about the image of the egg? The egg symbolizes birth and/or re-birth. In the case of Aristides, the unconscious is attempting to turn his attention towards something unknown to his consciousness. It is significant that there is a fourth mysterious egg which is given to him by a temple official. What does this fourth egg symbolize?[20]

If we accept the notion that Aristides' worship of Asclepius involved a certain amount of repression and sublimated energy then it appears that these repressed elements have a tendency to return into consciousness. The symbol of the fourth egg may represent this movement towards conscious realization of the repressed past. Aristides' devotion and love of Asclepius represents a compromise between the forces of the unconscious: his relationship with the god satisfied aspects of his psyche that were damaged in childhood yet this religious gratification is attained in a manner that still implicitly requires a definite amount of unconscious repression. The process of conscious awareness is never completed, as is evidenced by the fact that Aristides remains a hypochondriac throughout the remainder of his life. Although his problems lessen in magnitude, they do not dissolve once his religious relationship with his god develops. Rather, without his illnesses there would never have been a need for the god's cures and hence the religious relationship would have come to an end. Such a state of affairs implies that there is a negative side of Aristides' religiosity since it

---

[20] For an excellent discussion of the symbolic meaning of 'four' in dreams and myths, see op. cit., p. 240f.

feeds upon his physical maladies which were expressions of unconscious anxiety. Thus, many of the so-called painful remedies viewed by Dodds as expressions of unconscious hostility may in fact be a manifestation of anger originally directed at Aristides' father but are now re-directed towards Aristides himself.

Chapter Nine: Concluding Remarks

First and foremost, we have learned that Aristides was an unusually devoted worshipper of the healer god Asclepius. As a devotee in the cult of Asclepius, Aristides recorded his dreams in textual form and the existence of this text has given us the opportunity to learn about his religious relationship to his god and his experiences in the cult. In spite of certain psychological issues that existed in his life, Aristides was able to function more of less successfully in his society as a sophist of some repute largely because of the religious therapy provided by the cult of Asclepius. For this reason, it makes more sense to view his religiosity in positive terms. Rather than labeling him as the "anxious pagan" Aristides may be the "healthy-minded pagan."

If Aristides does represent an anxious pagan, it should be noted that he did in fact suffer from what could only be construed as psychosomatic ailments which, in turn, could be seen as symptoms of anxiety. Although Aristides may have had psychosomatic ailments and did not like to speak publically, he functioned as an active and respected member of his society, with the possible exception of the first two years of his illness when he gave up his professional career as a sophist and lived in or near the temple sanctuary. It was during this two-year period at Pergamum that Aristides vigorously pursued his dream quest; in some measure it resulted in a transformation in his personal identity since he emerged from this period with a renewed sense of direction and energy for pursuing the life of the sophist. His dream visions during this period undoubtedly played a significant role in the development of his psychological integration and fostered his sense of "special election" or being a "chosen one."

Although a modern psychologist might be tempted to identify Aristides as a neurotic and even inadvertently dismiss his religiosity, we should note that his peers may not have perceived him in the same light. Aristides was never able to completely rid himself of his psychological difficulties because without them there would be no impetus to keep his religious relationship with Asclepius alive. Despite these psychological issues, Aristides, the healthy minded sophist, was able to function successfully in his society as a person of some repute largely because of the "divine benefits" provided by Asclepius and he was able to tell us about these divine benefits by writing the *Sacred Tales*. As Timothy Luke Johnson states,

> this mode of religiosity is optimistic about the empirical world as the arena of divine activity. It is intensely pragmatic about the benefits the gods offer: salvation involves security and success in this mortal life.[1]

Seen in this context, Aristides was anything other than an "anxious pagan."

In studying Aristides' *Sacred Tales*, it does not make much sense to understand the text in purely literary terms nor is it correct to explain his religiosity away as a product of some deep-seated psychological structure of the mind. However, we have identified the socio-historical and psychological factors that affected the nature of Aristides' piety and its symbolic articulation in textual form. Aristides' religiosity manifested a number of identifiable literary and socio-historical elements of the collective macrocosm of his social world. Although the sophist was a unique individual possessing a variety of different tendencies and idiosyncrasies, he created his universe of meaning by internalizing a number of literary conventions.

In Part I we focused our attention upon the historical and literary factors impacting his piety. Our starting point was to establish the idea that Aristides' visionary experience is a viable instance of authentic religious experience and we noted several parallels between Aristides' religious experience and other examples of religious experience present throughout the religious traditions of the ancient Mediterranean world. If we did not consider his piety to be genuine, then there would be little point for us to conduct a psychological investigation of his dreams and visions. By means of a

---

[1] Johnson, *Among the Pagans*, op. cit., p. 50.

comparative analysis, we have argued that Aristides' religiosity is genuine. In the process of doing so, we have noted several morphological similarities as well as some concrete differences between the *Sacred Tales* and several other Christian and non-Christian writings. These parallels are of the phenomenological variety and do not indicate any kind of historical dependence of one text upon the other. On the one hand, Aristides' account of his life does not depict a "history of the soul" in the traditional sense of what one would expect when one encounters a typical modern autobiographical document. Unlike Christian autobiographers such as Augustine, Aristides' autobiographical writings do not display any moral awareness. On the other hand, we have been able to identify several interesting comparisons existing between Aristides' *Sacred Tales* and other pagan writings. Aristides was a pagan, so it stands to reason that appropriate material for comparison would come from the pagan world, and several significant parallels between Aristides' religious diary and other pagan writings were uncovered. Many of the typical features of ancient miracle literature were encountered in Aristides' religious diary. It is even possible to consider the *Sacred Tales* as an example of "aretalogy."

In Part II we examined the psychological dimension of Aristides' religiosity, assessing the numerical frequency of the various dream images appearing in the manifest contents of Aristides' dreams. The predominant dream imagery in Aristides' dreams are related to religious and medical themes and this initiated an exploration of the psychological function of the figure of Asclepius and the cult of Asclepius in Aristides' life. We examined Aristides' conversion experience and noted the differences between his conversion and Christian conversion. The personal and social upheavals in Aristides' life created for him a psychological crisis leading to his conversion. Although there is little doubt that Aristides' neurotic problems played a major role in his religious behavior as is evidenced in his ever-present psychosomatic ailments and the subsequent performance of various painful divine prescriptions, in general his religious behavior served a positive function in his life. As a sophist, Aristides was a functioning member of his society for most of his life and there is no doubt that his religious relationship helped him remain a contributor to Roman society.

Our last task in this psychological exploration of Aristides' religiosity was to identify the main conflict which plagued him. Exploration of the latent or hidden dimension of his dreams uncovered a pattern of attachment to authority and a fear of separation from his parents. Most likely, this infantile struggle was the origin of the problem which led him to seek attachment to his god, Asclepius.

This volume demonstrates the value of an interdisciplinary approach for studying a religious individual. Rather than viewing the *Sacred Tales* and the experiences described therein from a single scholarly perspective, we have presented a multi-disciplinary approach for understanding the text. We have identified various religio-historical influences upon the text and demonstrated that Aristides' religiosity has a number of analogues in the history of Greco-Roman religion. Furthermore, employment of psychological concepts has demonstrated that Aristides' religiosity was conditioned by a number of psychic factors, many of which are reflected in his dreams. The justification for interdisciplinary methodology in this study is directly related to the complex multi-dimensional nature of religion; religious texts and experiences are understood with more clarity and less bias by using a variety of methodological viewpoints. Each method functions as a complement for some of the limitations of the other methods. Unfortunately, previous studies of Aristides have not taken such an approach. In applying this multi-disciplinary approach to Aristides, we have discovered that his religious experience was conditioned by a variety of theological, historical, social and psychological factors.

BIBLIOGRAPHY

Angus, S., *The Mystery-Religions and Christianity*, second edition, (New York, 1925)
Baumgart, H., *Aelius Aristides als reprasentant der sophistichen rhetorikder zweiten jahrhunderts der kaiserzeit*, (Leipzig, 1874).
Behr, C. A., *Aelius Aristides and the Sacred Tales*, (Amsterdam, 1968).
Benedict, Ruth, "Anthropology and the Abnormal" in *Human Values and Abnormal Behavior*, ed. Walter Nunokawa, (Chicago, 1965), pp. 50–62.
Bonner, C., "Some Phases of Religious Feeling in Later Paganism," *Harvard Theological Review* (1937, vol. 30, n. 3), pp. 119–131.
Boulanger, A., *Aelius Aristide et la Sophistique dans la Province d'Asia*, (Paris, 1937).
Brown, P., *The Making of Late Antiquity*, (Cambridge, Mass, 1972).
Cumont, F., *The Oriental Religions in Roman Paganism*, second edition, (New York, 1956).
Dodds, E. R., *The Greeks and the Irrational*, (Berkeley and Los Angeles, 1951).
———. *Pagan and Christian in an Age of Anxiety*, (New York, 1970).
Downie J., *Professing Illness: Healing Narrative and Rhetorical Self-Presentation in Aelius Aristides' Hieroi logoi*, Dissertation, (Chicago, 2008).
Eggan, D., "The Manifest Contents of Dreams: A Challenge to Social Science," *American Anthropologist* (vol. 54, n. 4, 1952), pp. 461–465.
Festugiere, A. J., "L'Experience Religieuse du Medecin Thessalos," *Revue Biblique*, (1939, vol. 48), pp. 45–77.
———. *La Revelation D'Hermes Trismegiste*, 2 vols. (Paris, 1950).
———. *Personal Religion among the Greeks*, (Berkeley and Los Angeles, 1954).
Griffiths J. Gwyn, ed., *The Isis Book*, (Leiden, 1975).
Harris, W., *Dreams and Experience in Classical Antiquity*, (Cambridge Mass, 2009).
Harrison, S. J., "Apulieus, Aelius Aristides and Religious Autobiography," *Ancient Narrative*, (2001, v. 1), pp. 245–259.

James, William, *The Varieties of Religious Experience*, (New York, 1958). Mentor paperback edition.
Johnson, L., *Among the Gentiles: Greco-Roman Religion and Christianity*, (New Haven, 2009).
Kittel, G., ed. *The Theological Dictionary of the New Testament*, (Grand Rapids, Michigan, 1964).
Konig, C., *De Aristides Incubatione*, Dissertation (Jena, 1818).
Michenaud, G. and Dierkens, J., *Les Reves dans les "Discours Sacres" d'Aelius Aristides*, (Mons, 1972).
Miller, P., *Dreams in Late Antiquity: Studies in the Imagination of a Culture*, (Princeton, New Jersey, 1994).
Moore, P., "Mystical Experience, Mystical Doctrine, and Mystical Technique." In *Mysticism and Philosophical Analysis*, ed., S. Katz, (New York, 1978), pp. 101–132.
Musurillo, H., trans. "The Martyrdom of Saints Perpetua and Felicitas." In *The Acts of the Christian Martyrs*, (London, 1972), pp. 106–131.
Nock, A. D., *Conversion: The Old and the New in Religion from Alexander the Great to Augustine of Hippo*, (London, 1952).
———. "A Vision of Mandulis Aion." *Harvard Theological Review* 1934, vol.27, pp. 53–104.
Pascal, Roy. *Design and Truth in Autobiography*, (Cambridge, Mass., 1960).
Perkins, J. *The Suffering Self: Pain and Narrative Representation in the Early Christian era*, (London and New York, 1995).
Pernot, L. "The Rhetoric of Religion," *Rhetorica*, 2006, vol. 24, n.3, pp. 235–254.
Petsalis-Diomidis, A. *Truly Beyond Wonders: Aelius Aristides and the Cult of Asclepius*, (London, 2009).
Rosen, G. *Madness in Society*, (Chicago, Ill, 1968).
Russell, B. *The History of Western Philosophy*, (New York, 1946).
Smith, R. 1984. "Misery and Mystery: Aelius Aristides." In *Pagan and Christian Anxiety*, ed. Smith, R. and Lounibos, J., (Lanham, MD, 1984), pp. 28–52.
Spiro, M., "Religious Systems as Culturally Constituted Defense Mechanisms." In *Context and Meaning in Cultural Anthropology*, ed. M. Spiro, (New York, 1965), pp. 100–117.
Tiede, D., *The Charismatic Prophet As Miracle Worker*, (Missoula, Montana, 1972).
Wach, J., *The Comparative Study of Religion*, (New York, 1958): Columbia University paperback edition.
Weintraub, K., *The Value of the Individual*, (Chicago, 1969).

INDEX

ANCIENT SOURCES

Aelian
    Fragmenta 89, 73

Aelius Aristides
 Oration to Rome, 118
 Oration to Sarapis, 115, 118
 Sacred Tales
  I.1, 65
  I.1–4, 48
  I.3, 65
  I.4–61, 33
  I.6, 66
  I.7, 88, 139
  I.8, 56
  I.9, 137
  I.12–13, 141
  I.13, 137
  I.17–21, 98
  I.17–18, 142
  I.17–21, 98
  I.18, 106
  I.21, 134, 137
  I.22, 57
  I.23, 133
  I.28, 137
  I.32, 56
  I.33, 88
  I.36, 141
  I.36–40, 88
  I.42–45, 88
  I.46, 56
  I.46–49, 140
  I.54–55, 88
  I.57, 72
  I.61, 72, 75
  I.67, 65
  I.69, 133
  I.71, 105
  I.91, 137
  II.1, 65
  II.2, 75
  II.3, 65
  II.9, 11
  II.10, 75
  II.15, 65
  II.18, 75, 105, 107, 117
  II.22, 73
  II.24, 75
  II.28, 67
  II.30, 65
  II.32, 57
  II.34, 66
  II 41, 57
  II.47–48, 75
  II.55, 65
  II.60, 117
  II.65, 117
  II.82, 65
  III.3, 136
  III.4–5, 106
  III.13, 120
  III.21, 99
  III.46, 56
  III.47, 115
  IV.7, 67
  IV.17, 65

IV.39–40, 65
IV.50, 142
IV.51, 20, 56
IV.54, 134
IV.56, 57
IV.57, 105
IV.60, 105
V.55, 65
V.64, 57

Alexander Polyhistor
Collection on Marvels, 82

Anonymous
Apocryphal Acts of the Apostles, 73
Gospel of Peter IX.35–36, 38
The Martyrdom of Perpetua and Felicitas and the Vision of Satyrus III–XXI, 36–38
The Shepherd of Hermes, 4, 38
Aristeides Prolegomena, treatise B, 12–13
A Vision of Mandulis Aion, 36

Apuleius
Metamorphoses, XI, 41, 53–55, 61, 68, 107

Aristotle
De Somniis, 86
De Divinatione Per Somnum, 86

Artemidorus
Oneirocritica, 87, 89, 139

Augustine of Hippo
Confessions, II.4.9, 4, 33, 41, 43–47, 49, 53, 57, 113–114

Augustus
Res Gestae Divi Augusti, 33

Cicero
De Divinatione, Book I xxf, II, 85

Dio of Prusa
De Exilio, 118

Ennius
Annales, 85

Fronto
Letter to Marcus Aurelius, 84

Galen
Platonis Timaeum Comment Fragmenta 87, e5–88, b5
Corpus Medicorum Graecorum, supp1, (1934) 33, 125

Herodotus
Histories
II.141, 104
V.56, 105
VII.16, 106

Homer
Iliad
II, 23, 106, 199–200, 101, 732, 10
IV.194, 106
X.496–497, 104
Odyssey
IX.190, 65
IXX.47, 117

Iamblichus
The Mysteries of Egypt, III.2, 107

Jewish Pseudepigrapha
I *Enoch* 14:8, 38
Syriac Baruch, 38

Josephus
Life, 33

Lucian of Samosata
  Alexander the Quack Prophet, 83
  The Death of Peregrinus, 116
  The Dream, 33
  True History, 85

Marcus Aurelius
  Meditations
    II.17, 50
    IV.3, 4, 33, 41, 49, 50, 53, 58, 114

Marinos
  Vita Procli 31.42, 76

Maximus of Tyre
  De Diss. XI, III, XXXVII, 86

Plato
  Seventh Epistle, 33
  Phaedo 60e, 106
  Phaedrus 257c, 65
  Republic 571c–572b.26, 89

Phlegon
  On Marvels, 82

Philo of Alexandria
  Life of Moses, 62

Philostratus
  Lives of the Sophists II.9, 12–13, 33
  Live of Apollonius
    I.33, 65
    4.18, 68, 82

Plutarch
  De Genio Socratis 22, 107
  Perikles 13, 76

Porphyry
  De Mysteriis
    II.2, 107
    II.8, 54

Proclus
  Plat. Remp. I, 54, 107

Suidas
  Lexicographi graeci I, ed. Adler, p.353, 12

Synesius
  Letters, 34

Thessalos of Tralles
  Letter addressed to Caesar Augustus, Catalogus Codicum Astrologonum VIII (Cod. Parisinon) 3, 35–37, 151

Tacitus
  Dialogues, 135

Zosimus of Panapolis
  The Visions of Zosimus, 39

Zostrianos
  Nag Hammadi Codices
    VIII.1.10–29, 51

BIBLICAL REFERENCES

Genesis	20:3	106
Exodus	34:10	65
Deuteronomy	3:24	65
1 Kings	3:4	106
Daniel		38
Job	37:1	65
Matt	13:54	66
Mark	5:25–34	4, 71, 76
Luke	4:39	76
	5:26	76
	11:14	66
John	5:20	36
	7:3	21
	4:10f	65
Romans	7:7–25	51
Phil		3, 52
Revelation		38

GENERAL INDEX

Achaians, 104
Africa, Thomas, 130
Agamemnon, 104
Alcinous, 86, 117
Alexander of Abonoteichus, 83
Alexander the Great, 82
ancient autobiography, 29, 32, 49
   history of the soul in ancient autobiography, 49, 95, 114, 149
   religious autobiography, 28, 44
ancient biographies of Aelius Aristides
   Lives, 12, 33
   Aristeides Proleomena, 12–13
   Suda article, 12
anthropological method, 24, 123, 126, 132, 151, 153
   and the study of abnormal behavior, 59, 123–124, 151
anxiety dreams in the *Sacred Tales*, 22, 100–101, 137
Apollonius of Tyana, 62, 68, 82–83
Apuleius, 41, 49, 53, 55–56

aretalogy, 4, 29, 61–64, 69, 71, 78, 149
Aristides
   anxious pagan, 3, 22–24, 27, 42, 50, 147–148
   eccentric tendencies, 18, 25
   first encounter of Asclepius and conversion, 119
   homo religiosus, 59, 68, 90
   journey to Rome, 13, 72, 86, 118
   masochistic tendencies, 120–121
   narcissism, 117, 122, 141–142
   psychosomatic illnesses, 122, 124–125, 134–135, 147, 149
   sick soul, 3–4, 22–23, 27, 41–43, 49, 59, 95, 114
   special election, 56, 147
Aristotle (philosopher), 86, 88
Artemidorus, 4, 86–89, 96, 106, 129, 138–139
ascent in dreams, 143–144
Asclepius (god), 73–77, 79, 83–84, 86, 90, 95, 100, 103, 105, 107, 109, 112–122, 124, 126–127, 132–135, 138–142, 144, 147–

149, 152
asceticism, 52
Asia Minor, 12, 35, 111–112
astrology, 90
Athena (goddess), 56–57, 76, 100, 103, 105, 114, 117–118
Augustine of Hippo, 43–47, 49, 52, 114, 117, 152
authenticity of dream-accounts, 24, 38
baths and bathing, 52–53, 75, 88, 100, 103, 121, 134, 137–139
Baumgart, H., 16–17, 33–34, 151
Behr, C. A., 11, 64
Benedict, Ruth, 123
Bonner Campbell, 14, 21
Boulanger, Andre, 17, 54, 61–62, 151
Brown, Peter, 21, 52–53, 111–112
chronology in the *Sacred Tales*, 30–32, 48
Cicero, 33, 85, 88
Confessions of St. Augustine, 4, 33, 41, 43–47, 49, 53, 58, 113–114
conversion, 5, 13, 36, 46–47, 51–52, 113–114, 116, 149
cross-cultural study of dreams, 5, 97, 129–131
cults
    Asclepius, 40, 68–69
    eastern cults, 54, 82, 90
    Roman cults, 14, 58
culture/personality theory, 97
Cynics (school of philosophy), 116
daggers and knives in Aristides' dreams, 137–138
Demeter (goddess), 67
Deubner, L., 106

Dilthey, Wilhelm, 7–8, 25–26, 32
Diogenes (philosopher), 116
Dierkens, Jean, 13, 16, 121–123, 152
divination, 5, 87, 134
divine prescriptions, 5, 10, 22, 69, 71, 74, 76, 87, 114, 119, 124, 127, 149
divine benefits, as part of a typology of religious experience, 15
    Aristides as an example, 21, 45, 148
Domitian (emperor), 116
Dodds, E. R., 11, 17, 77, 106, 119, 120, 137, 145
    culture pattern dreams, 15, 22, 104, 107
    age of anxiety, 14–15, 21–22, 37–38, 82, 99, 137, 151
dream-epiphany, 96, 105
    god-sent dreams, 57, 64, 106–107
    religious and prophetic dreams, 11, 86–87
    significant versus insignificant dreams, 87, 106
    systems of dream interpretation in ancient literature, 4, 87
    Aristides' system of dream interpretation, 89
dream-like qualities of Aristides' dreams, 18, 35, 37
early Christianity, 21
ecstasy, 28, 36, 49, 73
Edelstein, Ludwig and Emma, 10–11, 64, 69–70, 73–74, 76
Eggan, Dorothy, 97–98, 101, 151
Egyptian religion, 11, 39, 105, 115, 133

Eleusinian Mysteries, 114
mystery terminology in the *Sacred Tales*, 4, 67
Eliade, Mircea, 115, 143
Epidaurian inscriptions, 61, 63, 69, 70, 124
Epidauros, 68, 74
Erikson, Erik, 5, 25–26, 110–112, 135
ethical ideas, 45
Eudaemon, (Aristides' father), 12
failure of doctors
 in curing Aristides, 4, 71, 73
 in Greco-Roman miracle stories, 73
 in the New Testament, 71
Festugiere, A. J., 14, 17, 19, 21, 35–36, 64, 78, 118, 151
foster fathers
 Epagathus, 32, 134
 Sabinus, 11
 Zosimus, 99
Freud, Sigmund, 130–133, 136–138, 140–141, 143
functional analysis of religion, 5, 109
Glycon (god), 84
gnostics and gnosticism, 51
gods of Olympus, 104
gospels, 38, 61, 65, 66, 68, 101
Grant, Robert, 82, 90
Greco-Roman culture
 religion, 39, 150
 child-rearing practices, 5, 134–135
Greco-Roman novel, 55, 81
Hadas Moses, 62
Harris, William, 18, 34–35, 129, 152
healing miracles, 83, 112–115, 120, 141–142
 miraculous healing, 114
 suddenness, 4, 76

rational healing, 116
healing rituals, 126
healthy-mindedness, 4, 41–42, 52, 59, 147
Hellenistic religion, 14, 40, 65, 69, 78, 81, 112, 116
Hellenistic world, 48–49, 82, 88, 91, 112, 124
Heracles (god), 65
history of religions, 28
Holmes, Brooke, 129
Husserl, E., 7, 25
hypochondria, 18, 121–122, 144
hysteria, 121
incubation, 10, 98, 126
id and superego, 129
individualism, 82
initiation, 22, 53–55, 67–68
interdisciplinary method, 24, 130, 150
introspective conscience, 51, 95
Isis (goddess), 11, 53–56, 67, 100, 103, 107, 114
Jaeger, Werner, 49
James, William, 4, 42, 57–58, 113
Johnson, Luke Timothy, 15, 18, 21, 45, 148, 152
Judaism, 39, 65, 113
Judeo-Christian religious tradition, 113
Jung, Carl, 39, 67, 143
Kee, Howard, 62
Konig, C. A., 16–17, 152
Kummel, Werner, 51
Liebeschuetz C., 84
life-cycle theory, 119
Lincoln, J. S. 131
Luther, Martin, 7–8, 25, 110
magical ideas, 53, 75, 81, 83, 86, 90, 141
Marcus Aurelius, 4, 22–23, 33, 41, 49–50, 52, 84, 135, 140

Malacarne V., 120–121
Malinowski, B. T., 132
medicine, 10–11, 43, 72–74, 120
Meditations of Marcus Aurelius (emperor), 4, 33, 41, 49–50, 53, 58, 114
Meier, C. A., 67–68
Michenaud, G., 13, 16, 121–123, 152
Miller, Patricia, Cox, 15–16, 152
Misch, Georg, 32–33, 48–49
mithraism, 114
Moira, 115
Moles, J, L., 116
Momigliano, Arnauldo, 32–33
morality, 46
Moses, 62
Muslim religious tradition, 114
Mysteries, 54–55, 68, 114
mysticism, 58
myths and rituals, 6, 24, 82, 85, 113, 144
Nestor, 104
Nilsson, Martin, 14, 62–63
Nock, A. D., 36, 67, 73, 113–114, 116, 152
Odysseus, 85–86, 117
Oneirocritica, 87, 89, 139
On Marvels, 82
Oracles, 28, 83–84, 89, 106
 of Delphi, 116
 of Trophonius, 107
Oppenheim, Leo, 77, 106
Otto, Rudolf, 68
paradoxical cures, 4, 72, 75, 119–120, 124
parallels between the *Sacred Tales* and miracle stories in the *New Testament*, 4, 61, 71
 with the *Metamorphoses*, 54, 58, 61, 68

Paul (saint), 47, 33, 49, 51–52, 114
Pax Romana, 111
Pergamom, 10, 20, 30, 63, 67, 73–74, 111, 126, 147
Perkins, J., 18, 42–43, 152
Pernot, Laurent, 31, 152
Perpetua of Carthage, 4, 22, 36–37, 40, 48, 98, 152
pessimism, 45, 49, 51
Petsalis-Diomidis, Alexis, 17–20, 152
phenomenological study of religion, 25
Plato, 33, 50, 62, 65, 89, 99, 102, 105–106, 125
psychoanalysis, 5, 24–26, 101, 121–122, 129–131, 136, 144
psycho-social theory, 5, 109, 111, 135
Pythagoreanism, 90
quasi-conversion, 5, 114, 116
religious adhesion, 5, 11, 117, 126
religious experience
 definition, 6
 reasons for the study of, 7–9
 functional analysis of Aristides' religious experience, 5, 109
 ineffability of religious experience, 40, 55, 78
 methodological questions about religious experience, 24–26
Religious exclusivism, 114–115
Religious fear, 66–68
Roman child-rearing practices, 5, 134–135
Rosen, George, 126, 152
Russell, Bertrand, 44, 152

Sacred Tales
   various translations of the title, 11–12
   religious elements, 12, 16
   rhetorical interpretation, 3, 16–21, 27, 31, 34
Sarapis (god), 11, 54, 63, 67, 100, 103, 114–115, 118, 133
Sartre, Jean Paul, 7, 25
Satyrus, 36–38
Schleiermacher, Friedrich, 7–8
Second Sophistic, 12, 17–18, 84
Seligman, C. G., 131
separation anxiety, 136
skepticism, 87
Smith, Morton, 62–63
Smith, Robert, 21–23, 46, 152
Smyrna, 12, 72, 111, 138, 142
Socrates (philosopher), 62, 116
Southey, Robert, 32
Sophists, 12, 19–20, 33–34
Sophocles, 99, 102, 105
Starbuck, E. D., 113
Stendahl, Krister, 51–52
stoicism, 49–50
symbol of the egg, 142–144
syncretism, 14, 68
Synesius, 33–34, 89

Telesphorus, 100
Theodorus, 56
Theological Dictionary of the New Testament, 54, 65–66, 68–69, 152
theological ideas, 12, 28, 30, 38, 44, 50, 150
theos aner, 4, 20–21, 27, 62, 83
Thesallos of Tralles, 4, 35–37, 151
Tiede, David, 62–64, 153
Tyche (god), 114
varieties of religious experience, 42, 57–58, 113, 152
visions, 11, 28, 29, 31, 36–40, 47–48, 50, 52, 55, 57–58, 67–68, 85, 90, 95, 99, 104, 107–8, 119, 121, 126, 147–148
Volgases, 99
Wach, Joachim, 6, 28, 153
Weinreich, Otto, 68, 75–76
Weintraub, K, 46, 153
Welcher, 34
Yeats, W. B., 58
Zeno (philosopher), 116
Zeus (god), 57, 63, 104, 118
Zosimus of Panopolis, 39

Lightning Source UK Ltd.
Milton Keynes UK
UKHW04n0935310818

327926UK00001BA/18/P

9 781463 202323